Europe's Dogs of War on the African continent
Ripping all to shreds

KAPUTALA

In the years of famine following World War 1 in East Africa two words were coined by the local people: *mutunya* and *kaputala*. *Mutunya*, meaning scramble, refers to the frenzy of the starving crowd whenever a supply train passed through. *Kaputala* refers to the shorts worn by the British troops: it was these soldiers, according to the local Gogo tribespeople, who were responsible for their plight.

KAPUTALA

THE DIARY OF
ARTHUR BEAGLE
&
THE EAST AFRICA CAMPAIGN
1916–1918

*To Rupert
With compliments
+ best wishes
Alan*

HAND OVER FIST PRESS

This book is for
my aunts, Ivy and Joyce,
and especially my mother,
Mary Valerie Rutherford.

I would like to acknowledge
the help of Anne Meilhon, Ivy Ravenscroft,
Ann Rutherford, Muriel Guy, Renzo Giani and
James Beckett Rutherford, without whom this project would be
lacking. I would also like to thank my daughters, Joanna and
Tanya, for reading the book for errors, and to Kirsten Robertson
who proof-read the book into shape.

This book is dedicated to all those
who have lost their lives in futile wars,
to all the decendants of Arthur Beagle,
to my family: Ann, my daughters Joanna and Tanya –
and especially my grandsons:
Callum, Cameron and Oscar.

In memory of my brother,
Brian David Rutherford,
gone, but never forgotten.

KAPUTALA

THE DIARY OF
ARTHUR BEAGLE
&
THE EAST AFRICA CAMPAIGN
1916–1918

Edited and Introduced by
Alan Rutherford

HAND OVER FIST PRESS

This edition published by Hand Over Fist Press, 2001

16 Longlands Road, Bishops Cleeve
Gloucestershire GL52 4JP

email: *glueyander.co.uk*
alan.rutherford@cableinet.co.uk

website:
~~http://handoverfistpress.webjump.com~~
www.handoverfistpress.com

KAPUTALA

THE DIARY OF
ARTHUR BEAGLE
&
THE EAST AFRICA
CAMPAIGN
1916–1918

ISBN: 0-9540517-0-X

Acknowledgement
Information in East Africa Campaign, 1916–1918 from
James Paul at http://british-forces.com

Arthur Beagle's photographs supplied by Ivy Ravenscroft.

This book printed by Antony Rowe Ltd,
Chippenham, England

CONTENTS

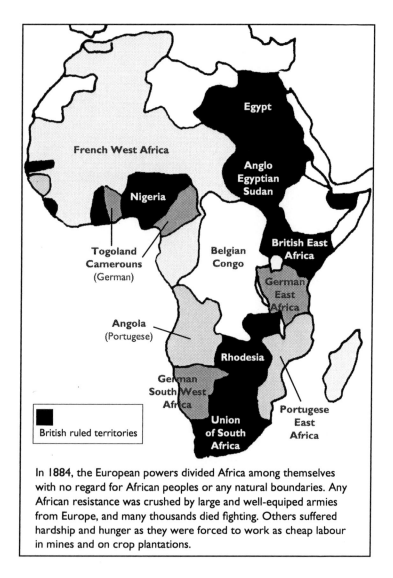

French West Africa

Egypt

Anglo Egyptian Sudan

Nigeria

Togoland Camerouns (German)

Belgian Congo

British East Africa

German East Africa

Angola (Portugese)

Rhodesia

German South West Africa

Union of South Africa

Portugese East Africa

British ruled territories

In 1884, the European powers divided Africa among themselves with no regard for African peoples or any natural boundaries. Any African resistance was crushed by large and well-equiped armies from Europe, and many thousands died fighting. Others suffered hardship and hunger as they were forced to work as cheap labour in mines and on crop plantations.

Africa: By 1914 seven European nations; Britain, France, Germany, Italy, Portugal, Belguim and Spain, had taken control of the continent.

INTRODUCTION

World War 1 was, as its title implies, a war which was fought worldwide and although the horrific slaughter in the trenches of Europe have been given top billing in historical accounts, other theatres of this war were no less barbaric. This book is based around a diary from November 1915 to August 1919 kept by my grandfather, Arthur Beagle, and covers his involvement in the East African campaign. In the diary place names have dubious spellings, his accounts are brief and he gradually slips into a spiral of fever attacks, but it contains interesting insights into this overlooked campaign, and confirms the tragic waste of life and the futility of warfare.

In the dying, glowing embers of the British Empire it would seem the greatest virtue of a soldier in 1914 was blind obedience; sadly human life was subordinate to God and King, and their accompanying jingoism. The 'Empire' was portrayed as a symbol of all that was most worthy of a man's sacrifice. The very notion of 'Empire' was still a magnificent facade of power that hypnotized both its subjects and its enemies – the map of the world was red from end to end even though much of that Empire had no idea how it came to be ruled by arrogant white men in baggy shorts. But being a part of it, it was said, 'distilled a kind of glory in the very beer of the average man'.

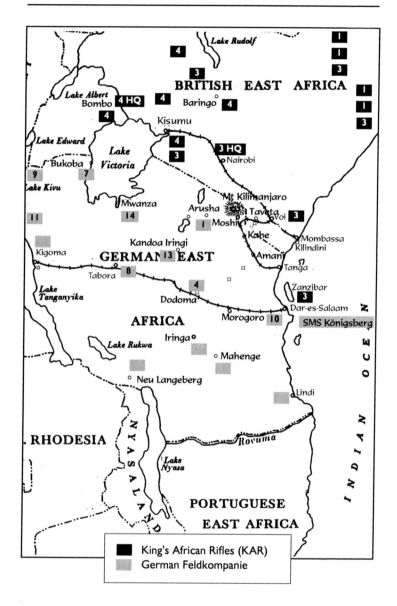

East Africa, 1914

Reasons for a world war in 1914 can be summarized
and credited to the spreading of competing industri-
alist nations across the globe. Original capatalist states
such as Britain, USA and France were joined by others
– Germany, Japan, Italy, Russia – in their hunt for gold
and slaves, oil and opium, colonies and cheap labour,
markets and strategic advantage. The competition
between them *gave* us the First World War. The same
development of industry which led to these imperialist rivalries ensured this war was the most bloody
which had ever been fought. Weapons of mass
destruction, unimaginable before the development of
industry, were now in the hands of jostling gangsters
and thieves – poised to kill millions. Tanks and
machine guns, gas and aircraft made this the first war
in which the majority of dead were the victims of other
soldiers, not of disease. The British alone lost 20,000
dead in a single day on the Somme and one million
killed in the four years of war. And if capitalist industry
caused the war it also had to keep the war going.
Directed labour, censorship, conscription and the
bombing of towns made this the first total war, a war
fought at home as well as on the battlefield.

And so in 1914, because of this imperialist rivalry; that
facade of Empire, *loyalty to the Crown*, was about to be
tested – 450 million people of every race and tribe, by
a single declaration of the King, were at war with
Germany. Unbelievably, banners and patrotic fervour
burst forth in a spirit of willing sacrifice impossible to
comprehend or even describe today.

In the days that followed that declaration, white men in
far-flung colonies of Britain and Germany, which had

coexisted, sometimes as intimate neighbours, eyed each other with newly found suspicion and then prepared to annihilate each other. South African forces were enlisted to capture German South West Africa and destroy the powerful wireless transmitters there. But before joining the war on the British side, South Africa's Premier Botha, and Major General Smuts, both former Boer War generals, had to put down an open rebellion in South Africa by units of their armed forces and some influential veterans of the Boer War who were totally opposed to anything 'British'. With the atrocities of South Africa's Boer War still fresh in the minds of the Afrikaans speaking population (Boers) some opted, quite understandably, to support Germany. The mutiny quickly dealt with, Premier Botha (once Commander-in-Chief of the Boer Army) returned to the field as General and led the South African and British forces, supported by Smuts, in a campaign which forced the surrender of the German forces in South-West Africa (now Namibia) in July 1915.

In East Africa, at the start of World War 1, the British controlled Zanzibar, Uganda, and what were to become Malawi, Zambia and Kenya; German East Africa (comprising present-day Rwanda, Burundi and Tanzania) was effectively surrounded and her troops outnumbered. The outcome should have been swift, but from the outset the British were thwarted by the inspirational leadership and military genius of General Paul von Lettow-Vorbeck, the German Commander-in-Chief, and the quality of the local Askaris (European-trained African troops).

Lettow-Vorbeck's philosophy was simple – by using hit-and-run tactics he would tie down huge numbers of

British troops in East Africa and so prevent them from joining the fighting in Europe. Prussian officers, contrary to the popular stereotype of rigid disciplinarians, were often quite the opposite, in fact some were extremely flexible and adaptable to their surroundings, and Lettow-Vorbeck was a marvellous example.

In East Africa for six to seven months each year the land remains parched and brown, starved for the moisture of the long rains which arrive in summer (November). Conditions were appalling; with temperatures often over 90°F, continuous rain for months on end and many poisonous insects and dangerous animals.

The landing of ill-prepared troops from India at Tanga was repelled with ignominy by the Germans in November 1914. Initially the British forces in East Africa were convinced that they would make short work of the Germans in Africa, but an underestimation of the enemy combined with very poor British command, and they were soon disillusioned. At Tanga, for instance, the Royal Navy had previously made a truce with the Germans and, chivalrously, they insisted that the Germans must be told if this truce were to be broken, thus telling the Germans that an attack on Tanga was imminent – so at one stroke, a major strategy of war, surprise, was sacrificed and in the battle that ensued the mould for future engagements under Generals Aitken and Stewart were set. Here simple principles of warfare were disregarded: intelligence diligently gathered by intelligence officers like Captain Meinertzhagen, one of the few British officers who had experience of East Africa, were haughtily ignored; the failure to make a reconnaissance

Wreck of the Königsburg in the Rufiji Delta, eventually destroyed by HMS Severn and HMS Mersey
Photograph: from the book *Tanganyikan Guerrilla*, Major J. R. Sibley, originally selected from the Bundesarchiv

dismissed as irrelevant. The lack of cooperation between the navy and the army leading to the lack of surprise – and the use of troops of questionable ability all gave victory to the Germans who were outnumbered eight to one. The ill-prepared Indian troops sent against them, were reduced, in the uncharitable words of one of their British officers, to 'jibbering idiots, muttering prayers to their heathen gods, hiding behind bushes and palm trees...their rifles lying useless beside them'. The battle was unique in that at one point a swarm of angry bees caused both sides to retreat in confusion.

For many, warfare in Africa was proving to be an unsettling experience, and worse was still to come. Although on the whole it was characterized by a relic of nineteenth century military etiquette, a ridiculous 'gentleman' code which never extended itself to the lower ranks. So that in Byron Farwell's book, *The Great War in Africa*, after the Battle of Tanga the officers of the German victors and British vanquished met under a white flag with a bottle of brandy to compare opinions of the battle and discuss the care of the wounded. Both sides exchanged autographed photos, shared an excellent supper, and parted like gentlemen.

One of the more riveting episodes of the war in Africa was that surrounding the destruction of the Königsberg, one of the German Navy's most modern and powerful ships. It was captained by Max Loof, who continued to fight on land after his ship had been destroyed. The Königsberg captured the first British ship to be taken in the war, and sank the warship 'Pegasus' within twenty minutes with 200 direct hits. Arthur Beagle mentions the wreck of the 'Pegasus' in his diary noting that 'this was the cruiser which was shelled...whilst cleaning out boilers and doing repairs.'

Ironically British ships finally pinned down the Königsberg well inland in the Rufiji Delta, where it had gone for overhauling and repairs: its engine had to be hauled to a machine-shop in Dar-es-Salaam, and back again, by thousands of African labourers. P. J. Pretorius, a famous Afrikaner hunter, was engaged to scout the network of rivers of the Rufiji and locate the warship. The story of this dangerous mission is told in his book, *Jungle Man*. Locating and destroying the

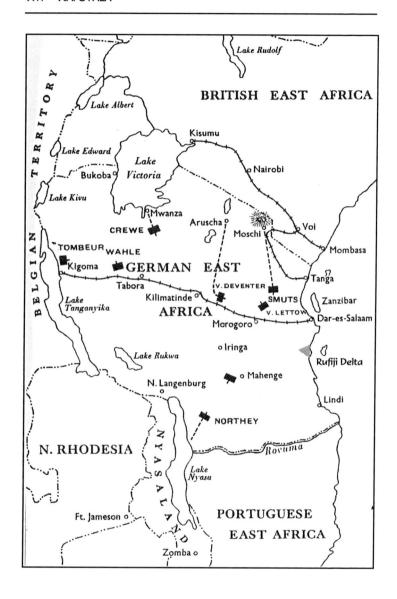

East Africa, July 1916

Königsberg was one of the most protracted engagements in naval history. In the steaming hot delta, the Germans, ravaged by disease, managed to evade and fight off the pursuing British forces for 255 days. It took a total of twenty-seven ships to destroy the German cruiser in a series of running battles on both land and water, and even then the German sailors escaped capture, taking the ship's 105mm guns with them.

In February 1916, at around the same time as Arthur Beagle began his diary, a new commander arrived in East Africa to pit his wits against the Germans: Jan Smuts, now Lieutenant-General Smuts. He tried to add new impetus to the British effort, immediately going on the offensive. He commanded a mixture of men and races from all over the Empire. A massive invasion from the north, comprising British and colonial troops under Smuts, was launched immediately, to be coordinated with a Belgian invasion from the west and with an independent British one from Nyasaland in the south.

The British and Germans employed African labour as 'support personnel' for battles in East Africa. In these overtly racist times 'support personnel' was a euphemism for exploitation; black people were treated like animals. Since campaigns here were fought in remote territory, military supplies were carried for long distances on the heads of hundreds of African porters to armies in the field. From an entire ship, dismantled, carried from the coast to Lake Tanganiyka, and there reassembled – to dismantled trucks, everything had to be carried. The deaths of many African carriers or porters, as well as fighting men, resulted from overwork and exposure to new disease environments, in fact deaths were so numerous, and recruitment to replace them so severe that a revolt occurred in Nyasaland in protest. Conditions for Africans were desperate, they were the fodder, to be used up and discarded.

Black South Africans were rightly wary and cautious of being involved in another 'white man's war' with the Boer War still a fresh memory, but they were coerced to enlist by officials desperate for African labour. So, for example, in the Mahlabatini and Harding districts of Natal the magistrates threatened to arrest and fine headmen who failed to produce a certain quota of recruits. Indeed, some recruiting agents became so desperate that, to the annoyance of the military authorities in East Africa, even children aged fifteen and sixteen and physically infirm Africans were signed up. Africans constituted almost one-third of the total number of South Africans (161,000 men) involved in the South West and East African campaigns. In terms of manpower it certainly was a significant contribution – one which received no recognition at the time and has subsequently remained largely ignored in South African history.

Despite his enthusiasm and eagerness to get to grips with what at times must have seemed a phantom enemy, Smuts met with little success.

Smuts' envelopment strategy was repeated time and time again – and always with the same result. His campaign in East Africa was a series of frustrating attempts to surround Lettow-Vorbeck's main force and bring him to a decisive battle. He never succeeded, each time the Germans eluded them, always retreating in the face of overwhelming force, but not before it was necessary. Smuts, and the commanders-in-chief who followed him, captured territory, but none succeeded in defeating the Germans.

Smuts, unhappy with the staff he had inherited, brought in two tough South African generals, 'Jaap' Van Deventer and 'Coen' Brits, both had fought the British in the Boer War. Upon being summoned to East Africa Brits cabled Smuts:

Mobilization complete. Who must I fight?
The English or the Germans?

Chasing Lettow-Vorbeck proved to be an agony of endurance for the Allied forces – and, unlike the European battlegrounds, here disease took a heavier toll than the enemy, and the conditions under which the troops marched and fought took them to the limits of human endurance. According to Byron Farwell, on one march 1,639 horses and mules died from the tsetse flies that swarmed in the bush, leaving a putrefying corpse every 100 yards of the route. The starving soldiers lived on paw-paws and groundnuts, struggling to move vehicles through the ever present mud, and often ended up lying helplessly in the mud 'retching from the stench of dead animals and watching the rats crawl over us...'

They suffered from ticks which caused fever, flies, dysentery, blackwater fever and 'guinea worms' whose millions of larvae spread through a human body to produce abcesses in the genitals, lungs and heart. It was impossible to remove the worms until they came to the skin surface, after which they could be pulled out, a few centimetres each day, taking care not to break them and release more larvae into the bloodstream. Jigger fleas, which burrowed into the troops' feet, caused agony and could only be removed with a needle or knife point. Every day the soldiers had to go through the ritual of removing them, on average twelve to forty per day. Some soldiers lost all their toes as the jiggers fed on the infected flesh of their feet.

Diseases like malaria and blackwater fever were rife, and disease made no distinction between Allied or German troops, or between black and white. All the troops in East Africa suffered from malaria, but blacks and whites did not suffer equally. Lieutenant-Colonel Watkins, director of the labour bureau for all military labour in East Africa stated at the end of the war, 'Where a Medical Officer had to deal with white and with black patients in times of stress, the latter suffered. In a word, the condition of the patient was apt to be a consideration subordinate to his colour...'

During the first four months of 1917, 1,600 of 2,000 men quartered along the coast in an area heavily infested with malaria succumbed to the disease, those that survived were often broken in health for the remainder of their lives and the fatalities did not end in East Africa either; of the 700 maleria cases on board the ship *Aragon*, 135 died before it reached Durban.

Aircraft of the Royal Flying Corps (RFC) were used for reconnaissance, and to 'bomb' the enemy on the few occasions that the pilots could find them. The bombing, however, was not very accurate. Characters like

'Karamojo' Bell, an elephant hunter, refused to fly with an observer because a second man in the plane would have blocked his view as he swooped down to blast away at the enemy with his elephant gun.... .

Lieutenant-General Hoskins took over as Commander - in-Chief in January 1917 when Smuts was appointed a member of the Imperial War Cabinet in London. Smuts' farewell comments were less than helpful and incorrect when he stated that with most of the German colony in Allied hands, the Germans had been defeated and all that remained was a little clearing up. In October 1917 the last big battle, and by far the bloodiest, was fought at Mahiwa – it was a set piece battle resembling those on the European front. Again the Germans managed to outwit the British, losing only ninety-five killed, whereas the British lost more than half their men – 2,700 out of a total of 4,900 men. Lettow-Vorbeck was forced to withdraw as his forces had by then been reduced to less than a thousand men.

With a series of skirmishes and ambushes, Lettow-Vorbeck led the British by the nose into Mozambique, where the Germans easily routed a numerically superior Portuguese force with contempt, and finally sneaking into Northern Rhodesia. Cut off from their supply lines the Germans lived off the land, using captured weapons and ammunition obtained along the way from well-stocked Portuguese supply dumps, and in spite of the hardship the morale of the German force was exceptionally high. Marching through strange lands far from home, often living under the most primitive conditions, without letters or news of any sort, isolated from any support, fighting and constantly retreating, with only the very faintest hope of a final victory, they all soldiered on. The morale of the British was, surprisingly, no less than that of the enemy as they struggled along behind.

Crossing into Northern Rhodesia Lettow-Vorbeck faced a force made up of Rhodesian police and civilian volunteers. It seemed likely that he would make his way South but, having captured Kasama, word reached him on 13 November 1918 that the armistice had already been signed and agreed in Europe. On 25 November, after confirmation that the war was indeed over, he surrendered, and his men laid down their arms.

The British officers, at last had the chance to meet the legendary general who had for so long managed to thwart their efforts to defeat the German army in Africa. Some openly admitted that they 'had more esteem and affection for him than for our own leaders'. The war, it was claimed (rather superciliously), had been fought in a gentlemanly fashion throughout, and Lettow-Vorbeck was not imprisoned, but given the use of a car and invited to dinner by Van Deventer.

With a force that never exceeded around 14,000 (3,000 Germans and 11,000 Askaris) Lettow-Vorbeck held in check a much larger force (estimates range from 130,000 to 300,000) of British, South African, Nigerian and West African, Indian, Rhodesian, West Indian, Belgian and Portuguese troops.

The aftermath of the war in Africa was more than just a matter of the jubilant victors and the honourably vanquished. The East African campaign left the country ravaged. More than 100,000 troops and tribespeople died as a result of the conflict, either during the fighting or from the subsequent famine. In Dodoma, for instance, reckless appropriation of the villages' grain supplies and cattle by both the Germans and British eventually led to the death of 30,000 Africans. Two words were coined by the stricken people during those years: *mutunya* and *kaputala*. *Mutunya*, meaning scramble, refers to the frenzy of the starving crowd whenever a supply train passed through. *Kaputala* refers to the shorts worn by the British troops. It was these soldiers, according to the local Gogo tribespeople, who were responsible for their plight.

In Dar es Salaam, surrounded by flowerbeds, is the Askari Monument. It bears the words of Lettow-Vorbeck:

'In memory of native African troops who fought,
To the carriers who were the feet and hands of the army,
And to all other men who served and
died in German East Africa 1914–1918,
Your sons will remember your name.'

The East Africa Campaign does at times, read like fiction – with warships doing battle inland, hundreds of miles away from the sea, zeppelins attempting to fly the 3,600 miles from Germany to East Africa with supplies, and a colourful mixture of brilliant soldiers, big-game hunters, frontiersmen, killer bees and tsetse flies all battling, for king or kaiser (and quite inexplicably), for possession of a vast tract of one of the most inhospitable parts of Africa.

Editors note

It may appear that certain sections within this intro-
duction and the concluding 'The East Africa Campaign,
1916–1918' give an impression of blasé 'matter of factness'
and that writing on particular campaigns may seem to
revel in the militaristic jargon of the source matter,
however it is not my intention to make light of war's
wretchedness and definitely not to promote militarism, in
fact quite the opposite. I hope all who read this account
will find war abhorent and feel a great sympathy for those,
black and white, forced, coerced or duped into the ranks,
for whatever reason – be it straightforward intimidation
or the sickly-sweet lure of drum-thumping jingoism.
Cutting away all the bullshit, no matter how 'gentlemanly'
the conduct of some officers, a lot of people died horrible
deaths because the greed of competing capitalisms could
not coexist on the same planet.

I cannot guarantee that Arthur Beagle would have agreed
with the anti-war slant of this book, but by all accounts he
was a kind and good man and I sincerely hope he would
have.

Alan Rutherford, 2001

Sources & Further Reading

I would like to acknowledge the help and assistance of Renzo Giani, who made these books available, and my sister Anne Meilhon, who copied and posted them to me. I also acknowledge, with grateful thanks, that the books below were sources of information used extensively in this book.

Brown, James Ambrose *They Fought for King and Kaiser*, South Africans at War Series, Ashanti Publishing (Pty) Ltd, 1991.

Farwell, Byron *The Great War in Africa*, W W Norton & Company, New York, 1989.

Grundlingh, Albert *Fighting Their Own War: South African Blacks and the First World War*, Ravan Press.

Pretorius, Major P. J. *Jungle Man*, George G. Harrap and Company Ltd, 1947.

Sibley, Major J. R. *Tanganyikan guerrilla: East African campaign 1914–18*, Pan/Ballantine, New York, 1971.

Relatively few books have been written on the subject of the African campaigns of World War 1 and even these do not remain in print very long. Most of them are written from a militaristic, matter of fact and unquestioning point of view which glorifies war and makes heroes of strategists. Farwell's book covers the fighting in Togoland, the Cameroons, SWA and East Africa.

They Fought for King and Kaiser is full of anecdotes and quotes from participants, but also some patronising material. *Tanganyikan guerrilla: East African campaign 1914–18* is the account I found most complete. The general impression of the Great War as a largely static war in which massive armies faced each other in trenches and slogged it out for months on end does not apply to the African theatres, these were campaigns of manoeuvre and guerrilla tactics, fought in bush, jungle and swamps.

Some other books currently still available on the East Africa campaign of World War 1 include *Military Operations, East Africa* (1941) by Lt Col. Hordern, a reprint of the HMSO official history, and *My Reminiscences of East Africa* (1920) by von Lettow-Vorbeck, a translation of the German general's memoirs. An excellent account, I'm told, now out-of-print and scarce, is *Battle for the Bundu* (1974) by Charles Miller. Also worth looking for is E. P. Hoyte's *Guerrilla* (1981), a book from the German perspective. Finally, *A History of the Kings African Rifles* by Malcolm Page.

Arthur Beagle
1887–1957

Photograph from around 1910

Arthur's parents, James and Mary Beagle, with grandson
Norman Beagle (son of C. Beagle mentioned on page 34).
Photograph taken around 1930.

Page from Beagle family bible, Arthur's parents marriage details
(page supplied by John Beagle)

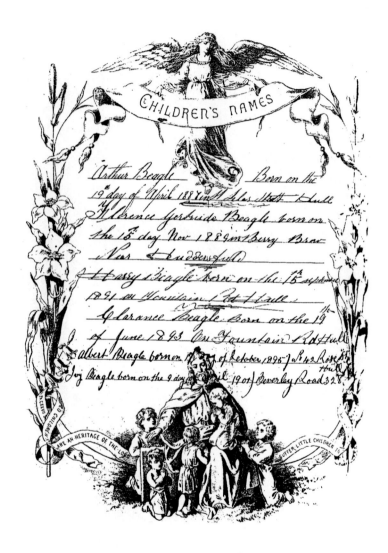

Page from Beagle family bible, birth dates of Arthur and his brothers and sisters
(page supplied by John Beagle)

Arthur Beagle (1887–1957)

My grandfather, Arthur Beagle, came from Hull, Yorkshire, where his father was a printer. He was one of seven children; in the back of the diary it mentions a C. Beagle 28th Squadron, Royal Flying Corps (RFC), Italian Exped. Force, and Ivy, Arthur's eldest daughter recollects one brother going to Australia and another to Canada. My grandmother's family, with the surname Guy, came from Keyingham near Hull, where her father was a carpenter. Jessica was one of fifteen children and twice a year her mother would take the whole family to Hull to be outfitted for summer or winter clothing. Ivy thinks it might have been on one of these visits to Hull that Arthur and Jessie met.

Arthur worked on outfitting the *Titanic* as a wheelright and carpenter before going on to work on the construction of a flour mill in Hull. From there he managed to get a contract to work on the building of another flour mill – this time in Senekal in the Orange Free State, South Africa. While working in South Africa World War 1 broke out and he enlisted in the Mechanical Transport and then with South African Horse 1st Mounted Brigade.

Jessie Guy, around 1910

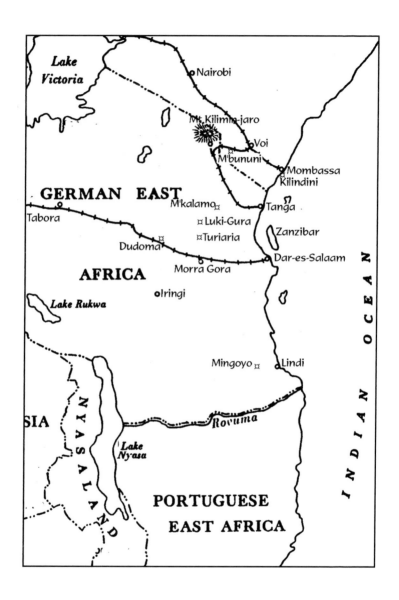

Arthur Beagle's East Africa, 1916-1818. The dubious spelling of place names intact.

The Diary of Arthur Beagle

20 November 1915 – 19 August 1919

Nov 20th Enlisted in Mechanical
1915   Transport as driver and
         was sent into fitting shops
         as mechanic in the E.D.F
         shops. Reg no 353

Feb 11th Discharged through demob-
1916   -ilization of the Unit

Feb 17th Re enlisted in the South
1916   African Horse 1st Mounted
         Brigade Reg no 2492

April   Transferred to the 2nd
15th   Mounted Brigade Train
1916   South African Horse as
         Wheeler on Mule convoy.

April   Left Robert Heights for
25th   British East Africa via
         Durban.

April   Left Durban for Mombasa
29th   on the St Egbert (which

Page one of the diary

THE DIARY

1915

Nov 15 Enlisted in Mechanical Transport as driver and was sent into fitting shop as mechanic in the U.D.F. shops. *Reg no 353.*

1916

Feb 11 Discharged through demobilization of the unit.

Feb 17 Re-enlisted in the South African Horse 1st Mounted Brigade. *Reg no 2492.*

April 15 Transferred to the 2nd Mounted Train South African Horse as Wheeler on Mule convoy. *Reg no 1491.*

April 25 Left Roberts Heights[1] for British East Africa via Durban.

---

[1] **Roberts Heights** from *They Fought for King and Kaiser*, James Ambrose Brown, 1991. Winnie Simpson recalled a scene in her memoirs as she saw it as a child of seven:
Few families were not affected. All military service was voluntary, and the men signed on for a campaign at a time. Early in 1915 daddy joined the local Citizen's Voluntary Training Corps. They drilled in the Market Square. Alongside of daddy's love of his family and devotion to home life, he was very strongly a born soldier. A mounted regiment was raised and N.2 Troop, A Squadron of the 1st South African Horse was recruited from Roodepoort, with our school principal, Mr Carter, as the lieutenant in charge of it, and the major was a Mr Stewart (Mudguts) from Krugersdorp. The training was at Roberts Heights, and there were few weekend passes. Mother went to Pretoria to meet him before the regiment left. Mother must have been very heavy-hearted as the time for departure drew near, but she was as brave as everyone had to be. When daddy left by train for Roodepoort I earnestly begged him to stand behind a big tree while shooting Germans, and just put his rifle round.

April 29   Left Durban for Mombasa on the St Egbert (which was captured by the German raider Emden[2] and after a few days of captivity was set free with the crews of condemned ships). On this ship we carried 950 horses and mules for the front.

May 6   Arrived off Kilindini,[3] 3 miles from Mombasa. We landed the animals after 3 days hard work transferring to lighters by slings. Had very narrow escape of being kicked overboard by a mule.

May 9   Left Kilindini in cattle trucks for the depot, proceeding through country covered with bush and jungle.

---

[2] **Emden**. The German raiders operated in all oceans at the start of WW I, using the strategy of terror amongst defenceless merchant shipping – usually sinking large numbers but occasionally capturing them for their fuel and provisions, as seems to be the case with the St Egbert. Karl von Müller, captain of the Emden, raided in the Indian Ocean and after 2 months of unparalleled havoc she was chased aground off the Cocos Islands by HMAS Sydney in November 1914.

[3] **Kilindini** from *They fought for King and Kaiser*, James Ambrose Brown, 1991 As a veteran of South West Africa Private F. C. Cooper noted the contrast from the landing on 'the inhospitable sands of Walvis Bay to the forests of coconut palms' as the infantry troopship nosed up the narrow channel to Kilindini harbour. They had been seven days at sea, crammed into the steamy messdecks.
He and his comrades, after unloading regimental kit and stores, explored the ancient Arab town with its British additions in the form of 'some good government buildings, private residences and shops, as well as a cathedral of oriental architecture'.
After one night under the tropical stars they were packed into trucks. 'The oven like bogies were shared with thirty-nine others, fly-bitten horses, sparse battery mules, solid-tyred motor lorries and Swahili stretcher boys.' More than half the men had to make the journey up-country standing. The train began its long climb through forests of coconuts and bananas, wrote Cooper. These gradually yielded to rubber plantations and fields of maize. 'We climbed steep gradients at a walking pace and rushed down inclines with a reckless speed that would have blanched the hair of a Cape branch-line passenger.' At the bottom of many a hill lay derailed trucks...

Quartered on deck aboard troopship
Photograph: Arthur Beagle

May 10 Arrived at Machoto and got the first glimpse of Kilimin-jaro,[4] the largest mountain in Africa. It is 19,700 ft high and it was around here that the North Lancs suffered heavy losses which resulted in the recalling of a General. We remained here four days and I was told off on grazing guard I had a good opportunity of getting into the bush where the game was plentiful although very difficult to shoot on account of the density of the bush. At night time the lions roamed round the camp quite near, within a hundred yards in fact.

May 15 Arrived M'bununi, the big base camp where all kinds of troops were gathered. On the first day I walked over to the camp of the 38th Howitzer Brigade which was formerly on Hedon race course. As nearly all the men were from Hull and only out from home three months I was very pleased to have a chat with them. Here I met the Roydhouses from Key.[5] We have 18 aeroplanes here with no opposition against them as the Germans supply of petrol has been exhausted. News came through that Van de Venter, the commander of the 1st Brigade has been surrounded and reinforcements are proceeding. Next day after six hours trek

[4] **Kilimin-jaro** *(Mount Kilimanjaro)* By the late nineteenth Century all the major geographical features had been explored by many European nations and their interest now focused on the political and economic advantages to be gained by establishing footholds in such an inhospitable corner of the world. Britain, France, Germany, Portugal, Belguim, Spain and Italy laid claim to vast territories on the African continent. British and German East Africa's border was a straight line from south of Mombassa going north-west to Lake Victoria, until, incredibly, Mt. Kilimanjaro was given by Queen Victoria to her grandson, the Kaiser, as a birthday present!

[5] **Key** Probably Keyingham, in Yorkshire, where my grandmother's family lived.

Arthur (right) and friends
Photograph from Arthur Beagle's album of the East African Campaign

they came back, have lost their way. An airman fell today and was killed, this making the fourth smash.

May 20 Railway line at Voi which is behind us has been blown up so it is evident the enemy has been through our lines. This would not be difficult as the bush is so thick round here.

May 29 Killed deadly snake in the tent. This camp is infested with all sorts of creeping and flying insects such as kaffir gods, locusts, beetles of all kinds, scorpions as large as crabs whose sting is almost as bad as a snakes, several cases have been fatal. Lizards and chameleons are to be seen everywhere. The latter is very pretty and change into any colour instantaneously. This country has a bad reputation for fever although at this time of the year the climate is at its best. I felt it coming on last night but it seems to be passing away now. News has come through that the 1st Brigade are hard pressed and living on quarter rations. Their clothes are in rags and they are cutting up their saddle flaps for slippers as their boots have worn away.

June 2 We are still at base camp and we all are impatient to be on the move. Horse and mules are dying fast although this is a healthy part of the country. One of our chaps has just caught a centipede under his blanket this morning. It was about 6 inches long and black with about 14 claws on its body. If these things put their claws into you its a case for the blanket and a firing party as a rule. I decided to inspect mine straight away and discovered two horrible spiders which are nearly as deadly. This country is giving me the creeps.

June 18   We have just struck camp and have got rations for a two month trek. We start out at 2 o'clock.

June 19   I have just laid out my blanket under a wagon and I feel about beat. We trekked all through the night with a halt occasionally to water the horses and mules. We passed the fly belt[6] during the night and arrived at this camping ground at 9 o'clock this morning. I had a trying time with my horse as he was fresh and rather festive but towards morning he became used to things. The country was picture to see at day break. We had entered a great open plain and in the distance was a range of mountains for which we were making, on our left was a fine forest. On the roadside we passed a dead giraffe, probably shot by some of our own fellows in front. On arriving here at Tsame the first thing I did was to off saddle and walk my horse two miles to water, over boot tops in dust. I then stripped and removed three ticks which had fastened on to my body and removed about a lb of baked sand and dust, in fact I looked like a nigger. By the way we have drawn rations for 4 days: 8 hard biscuits, 2lbs flour, tea, coffee, sugar, bacon and lime juice.

[6] **fly belt** Tsetse fly, African bloodsucking flies which transmit sleeping sickness in humans and a similar disease called nagana in domestic animals. Tsetse flies readily feed on the blood of humans, domestic animals, and wild game.

June 24   We have now been on trek seven days and I have had little chance of writing anything. We are about 80 miles from M'bununi and right in the heart of tropical country. This means trekking through thick bush covered with vegetation and creepers which makes progress impossible until you cut your road through. At present we have a good stretch of road in front of us, but for the last 30 miles the road has been very bad. One wagon was almost over the precipice and it took us 4 hours to get our 23 wagons through that gap. In some places there is a sheer drop of 500 ft where the road is cut round a mountain side. The dust is so thick that at times one can just see the outline of the horse and rider in front and we ride many a mile with our eyes closed and a handkerchief tied round the mouth. We did a hard day's trek yesterday and kept on through the night as we are pushing on to the German bridge at Railhead. I have never known what it was like to be hungry before but since we have been on this trek I have learned to enjoy crumbs of hard biscuit found in the bottom of my haversack. Our sergeant has just shot a buck so we look like getting some game before long. He also put 3 shots into a giraffe but it got away in the bush. We passed some good crops of cotton, tobacco and coffee but we have got orders not to touch any of it, as it belongs to peaceful natives. There are a good many tribes up here. Swahiles and Kaffirandies seem to be the most prominent. We see many of them wandering about with bows and arrows. The women do all the work.

Photographs: Arthur Beagle

June 25   We are now outspanned[7] at German bridge in Railhead and have just been down to the river for a bath. I should have had a swim only the river happens to be alive with crocs. We are giving the animals a rest here for 18 hours and as the roads in front are reported very bad they will need a rest. I feel down right sorry to hear the mules groaning, and although it seems cruel to drive them so, there are men in front badly in need of supplies. When a mule drops in his tracks he is just dragged into the bush at the roadside and the team made up again.

June 27   We inspan[8] this afternoon and from now on we trek at night and rest during the heat of the day until we catch up the Brigade which has just been in action. We heard that they have had 60 casualties.

June 29   Arrived Brigade HQ and camp here for about a week until supplies come up. This place is M'kalamo although there is no sign of a native hut even. We are making this place a supply base and I hear they are bringing a million pounds worth of supplies here.

June 30   Just got orders to saddle up and bring in a wagon which has smashed through the mules taking fright at a lion. I don't feel too pleased at the job as it is 8 o'clock at night and we have to go through thick bush. The

---

[7] **outspan** Boer *vortrekker* term for unharnessing animals and arranging the wagons in a defensive circle.

[8] **inspan** Boer *vortrekker* term for harnessing animals and preparing to move on.

sergeant, myself and 3 niggers are going. To make matters worse the roadside is strewn with bodies of horses and mules and the stench is something terrible. Every time my horse spots one of these bodies he tries to bolt and it takes me all my time to hold him. The officer tells me that we have lost 400 horses and mules already since leaving M'bununi. There are a few hundred men down with fever and dysentery.

July 4   Have just got orders from the Major to proceed 20 miles ahead and get some pumps working at the water holes. I am taking 2 natives and rations for 10 days.

July 6   Arrived Umbarque yesterday and have got two pumps working. Its a disheartening job. I have pumped one hole dry and water will not come fast enough so I shall have to do a little prospecting and dig for likely water holes. The animals are almost mad for water and its impossible to hold them back when they smell water.

July 8   I have been here four days and am having a quiet time. I have pitched camp in a little clearing in the bush with the 2 native boys for company. The sky is my roof of course and its rather lonely, but am enjoying the change. It seems like a picnic until I come to the evening meal which consists of mealie pap. I went out to get a shot at something but game seems to have been scared away, although four lions were sighted and also the spoor was there at the water holes.

July 10   Just received orders to pack up pumps and get away to Handini to catch up with the Brigade at the front. Snipers are busy along this road and one driver was shot.

July 12   Arrived at Headquarters at Luki-Gura. We are just behind the enemy now. In fact we are held up, there is nothing to see here beyond burnt out native huts. Throughout the whole of the trek we have not passed through a German town or village. We are now 300 miles from M'bununi and we have got to shift the German from his position in the mountains before we advance. The aeroplanes are continually going over but the enemies guns are so cleverly hidden that they cannot locate them.

July 17   The German big guns[9] were hard at it yesterday. I am at present on my back in hospital.

July 20   I am feeling better now but very weak. I have had 3 injections in my arm.

July 22   Feeling better again this morning but was pretty bad last night. Temp. 104.2. Sickness is very bad here. Hundreds of our chaps are down with fever and dysentery and hospitals are full. We, of course, do not get beds here, we just put our blankets on the ground and get down to it. The food has a good deal to do with all this sickness. We never get any

---

[9] **German big guns** 105mm guns removed from the destroyed German cruiser, Königsberg, by the crew, who avoided capture, taken inland and now deployed by Lettow-Vorbeck. These guns were to play a major role in the land battles that followed.

vegetables. A scout was brought in yesterday shot in the arm with a soft nosed bullet. He kicked out this afternoon. We are getting short of supplies as transport work is so difficult. One of our convoys came in last night after having a rough time. One team of mules were blown up along with the wagon and drivers by road mines. Another trooper was killed along with a corporal and three native drivers. I should have been with this convoy had I been well. One of our fellows saw the remains of a trooper partly eaten by wolves. They had practically dug him out of his grave which is barely below the surface as a rule. Cigarettes are very scarce here, seven rupees for a packet of 10, 1 rupee for a biscuit, 3 rupees for a 6oz bag of tobacco.

Aug 2   Down again with fever, this makes the third dose. The rainy season is coming on and as we have not tents, things do not look promising. We have been continually shelled this last week. They were at it all last night and our guns are outranged.

Aug 8   We have cut a new road to out flank the German position and we move off today.

Aug 10   We have got as far as we can along this new road and it is impossible to get wagon or anything else through excepting pack mules. The regiment have managed to scramble over the rocks taking ammunition and a few supplies with them. We along with the gun batteries have to return to the place we started from.

Aug 12   We are on the road again and proceeding to the nek where the German stronghold was. It appears the regiments that pushed on after we were left, attacked them in the rear which caused them to evacuate their position. Otherwise they would have been cut off.

Aug 13   We have passed through the nek the Germans held and we have got them on the run. We are making for Morra Gora and the railway. We have trekked 500 miles and it is 85 miles to the railway.

Aug 17   Arrived at Turiaria and are close on the Germans. I don't suppose I shall be able to go on any further. I have been sick on a wagon for 2 days and that alone is enough to break every bone in your body.

Aug 24   I had to go into hospital at Turiaria as I had a bad attack of fever, I was transferred to the clearing hospital on a lorrie 60 miles back on the line.

Aug 30   Discharged from hospital today to the detail camp. I am still weak as I have been rather bad and outside its simply pouring with rain, there is little shelter outside and we have to cook our own food which is fresh meat and flour.

Sept 5   Am feeling fit once again and have just come in from trench digging. I was on sentry last night.

Sept 9   I have been trying to get back to the Brigade but as the roads are too bad for transport I cannot get to them. I expect they will be 200 miles away by this time. I went to see the

C.O. of the 18th M.A.C. and he has allowed me to be attached as a fitter to the M.A.C. until I can join the regiment.

Sept 20　This life is quite a change to what I have been used to. I have a tent to sleep in and a stretcher bed to lie on. The food is also cooked ready for us, so I consider myself lucky. The cars are all Fords and there is always plenty of work. Of course they are all ambulance cars. One has just been blown up with a road mine, and a young driver with it.

Photograph: Arthur Beagle

Bottom photograph shows 'motor lorry converted to tractor for service on railway' (see opposite).

Photographs: Arthur Beagle

Nov 6   We leave today for Morra Gora and we expect to take three days to do the 150 miles.

Nov 8   We are having a good run and tonight we are parked up at the Warnie river. It appears our brigade was in action here just after I left for hospital and a big mistake was made resulting in the main body of the enemy escaping. In fact if things had gone right the war out here would have been over.

Nov 10   Arrived in Morra Gora, the first German town I have seen. This morning I went to report to the Major on the M.B.T. and he informed me that we have been disbanded and most of the men sent back unfit. As I am fit he is getting me transferred to the Mechanised Transport.

Nov 11   I have been transferred to the S.A.S.C.M.T. *reg no 3321*, and I rank as a driver. I am in the workshops now and if I pass the efficiency test which is a months probation I rank as mechanic with an extra 2/6 per day. Our work is to convert motor lorries into tractors for service on the railway.

Nov 28   Arrived at Dudoma 150 miles inland on the Tabora line. Was very glad to leave the last place as it was very hot and men have been going down fast with Blackwater.

Dec 3   Just heard of the Arabic going down with 7 weeks of our mail. It seems the letters are allowed to accumulate, so this must account for the long intervals between receiving letters.

Dec 23   In hospital with fever.

Dec 25   Xmas day and just had a quinine injection.

Wreck of the *Arabic*
Photograph: Arthur Beagle

1917

Feb 11   Still here in Dudoma with plenty of work. Sometimes we are at it until midnight from seven in the morning. The derelicts and convoys are coming in fast as the rains are coming on. In fact they have left it too long. One convoy took six weeks to come 50 miles and it meant hard work at that. Thousands of native carriers are now carrying the loads and the death rate is 40 per day on an average. Its awful to see them struggling knee deep in mud with a load on their heads. Further along the road among the mountains they are chained together as several of them have thrown themselves over the precipice.

April 11   I have been confirmed a mechanic to date as from Dec 12 at 9/6 per day. I was given to understand it was 12/6 but this rate has been altered by act of parliament. I have received a letter of yours from home regarding a speech of Gen. Smuts. He gave an account of hardships endured by troops out here. He has evidently given a vague idea as to the sufferings of sickness and starvation. The mounted men certainly had the advantage of the infantry as they were always in front and any food that was going was snapped up by them. The sufferings of infantry men have been terrible.

A chum of mine, late of the 7th Infantry tells me the following: *'After clearing out the Germans from Kilimin jaro region we had 26 days of continuous rain with one day fine. During this time we had no tents and the rations consisted of 1 cup of flour and a piece of buck. As we had to march from sunrise to sunset and the roads were one mass of slush there was little chance of getting dry wood to make fires with to cook food. We mixed water with the flour and drank it. Some time later the rations consisted of about 9" of sugar cane, one sweet potato and occasionally a spoonful of honey for 24 hours. We had no supplies for six weeks except what we got from the natives on the way side. Many of us marched in barefeet for miles and also did picket. One man was discharged from the field hospital as fit and was dead next day, and this is by no means an isolated case as scores have died of pure neglect.'*

April 28   Arrived at Ruivie Top along with four mechanics. This place has a bad reputation for fever. We have travelled about 300 miles from Dudoma, partly by train and the rest by road convoy. This is very mountainous country and in wet weather the roads are very dangerous as there are frequently drops of a thousand feet from the road side.

May 8   Got a slight touch of fever. Every morning there is a long line of men outside the hospital. In one month 350 men reported sick and the camp comprises that number coming and going.

June 26   Arrived in Dudoma again. We came 140 miles in a cattle truck 18 men and kit in each truck.

June 29   Sent out on lorrie convoy as driver. This work is very trying in the sun as there are no canopies on the lorries.

July 10   Back at No. 4 Workshop again. Some of my chums have been sent up to Iringi. From there they proceed to the mountains and dismantle Ford cars. They have to get the parts into 60 lb weights as near as possible for the natives to carry them 40 miles across these mountains and then connect up again to run on the plains at the other side where the Germans are being closely followed.

Photograph: Arthur Beagle

Photograph: Arthur Beagle

1918

Feb 16 Left for Dar es salaam and a prospect of trucks for a couple of days or more. 250 mile journey.

Feb 20 Am working in Base shop, engine dep. The heat here is something awful and the workshop is like an oven. Everything is strictly regimental here, what we South Africans have not been used to for some time.

March 22 Left Dares on draft for Lindi via Port Amelia which latter place is in Portuguese Africa. 1,300 miles.

March 8 Arrived at Lindi and reported to hospital to have tonsils cut out.

March 28 Discharged from hospital and am proceeding up the line to Mingoyo, another place with a fever reputation.

April 8 I have been working here in the shops but am feeling ill again.

April 10 Am in hospital again.

April 18 Discharged from hospital and going back to shops.

April 26 Back in hospital again, bad attack of fever.

May 3 I am still in hospital although removed to Lindi by river boat. I am feeling pleased today as the M. O. is evacuating me. It is now a matter of waiting for the hospital ship.

May 16	Arrived at Dares salaam on the hospital ship "Ebani" and admitted to hospital. Small pox broke out on the ship and all of us were vaccinated. (450 miles)
May 18	Yesterday I had another attack, temp. 104.6
May 25	Arrived at Dudoma. Convalescent camp from DSM hospital (250 mile journey).
June 14	Back in hospital again, malaria fever.
June 24	Evacuated again to DSM (250 miles).
July 4	Marked for Nairobi hospital.
July 7	Arrived Kilindini (150 miles by water).
July 9	Arrived Nairobi (750 miles)
July 24	Discharged to Detail camp.
Aug 1	Back in hospital with fever.
Aug 17	Discharged to Detail camp.
Aug 27	On draft for DSM.
Aug 29	Arrived Kilindini.
Sept 2	Embarked for DSM.
Sept 4	Arrived DESM via Zanzibar.
Sept 6	Admitted to hospital, malaria and bronchitis.
Sept 23	Discharged to Detail camp (Sea View).
Sept 26	Drafted to Base shops.
Oct 2	Admitted to hospital, bad case of malaria.
Oct 16	Had Medical Board and passed for

invaliding to South Africa as chronic malarial case.

Oct 26   Spanish Flu broken out.

Nov 1   Embarked on hospital ship "Gascon" for Durban. We call at Zanzibar which is 40 miles N.E. of DSM, also we pick up invalids from Beira. The journey is 1,700 miles. The wreck of the Pegasus is still in sight off Zanzibar. This was the cruiser which was shelled by the Germans whilst cleaning out boilers and doing repairs.

Nov 6   Arrived at Beira. We dropped anchor out at sea. This is a very difficult harbour to navigate into and after picking up the Pilot it took us $1^1/_2$ hours to get within the harbour.

Nov 9   Arrived at Durban and transferred to No 3 General Hospital.

Nov 23   Arrived at Wanderers Hospital, Jo'burg. Have been transferred as emergency case.

Dec 11   Am down with fever, the first attack since arrival.

Dec 31   Fever again.

1919

Jan 6	Am being transferred to Pretoria Hosp. for dental treatment.
Jan 20	Another attack of Fever. I have been advised to take Kharsivan treatment.
Mar 4	Discharged with 3 months leave.
Mar 31	Commenced work at Pretoria munici-pality. Same day attack of fever.
April 14	Attack of fever.
April 17	Started work.
May 19	Attack fever.
May 21	Started work.
June 2	Fever.
June 4	Started work.
June 16	Fever
June 18	Started work.
Aug 15	Flu
Aug 19	Started work

The diary ends here.

Postscript to Diary
After the war Arthur Beagle stayed on in Pretoria, sent for
Jessie, they married and had three daughters, Ivy, Mary
and Joyce – who gave them eight grandchildren.

Arthur managed several quarries: the Municipal Quarry
at Bon Accord in Pretoria until and during World War
Two; and later another at Bellville in the Cape. Bon
Accord was near Wonderboom air base and his daughters
helped out at the NAAFI. This was where my mother,
Mary, met my father, James Rutherford who was stationed
at Wonderboom with the RAF. Arthur played the violin,
golf and bowls, and he was a member of the Free Masons
and also a 'Moth'. He also had a spell at a pottery factory
in Olifonteins before retiring to Winklespruit on the Natal
coast.

I remember him with great fondness; driving around in a
black Plymouth, mints in the glove compartment, pipe
smoking, Xmas holidays, playing draughts, working with
wood and buying me my first bicycle.

Bill Ravenscroft married Ivy and they had three children:
Clive, Guy and Janet. James Rutherford married Mary
and they had three children: Alan, Anne and Brian. Clive
Warren married Joyce and they had two children: Russell
and Jeffrey.

Arthur Beagle died on 14 November 1957 in Winklespruit,
Jessie died on 10 February 1981.

Muriel Guy, Jessie's neice, says Arthur's sister, Ivy
Rogers, lived in Bridlington where she had a furriers.

ADDRESS

presented to

A. BEAGLE, ESQ.

Resident Manager, Municipal Quarry, Bon Accord.

SIR,

ON behalf of the Bantu employees of the Municipal Quarry, Bon Accord we, the undersigned, respectfully express our deep appreciation of your interest in our general welfare.

YOU have been instrumental in bringing about improvements in our housing and in the provision of better facilities. With the appointment of orderlies serving in a well equipped Clinic and also the appointment of a Bantu Overseer for our Compound, there is marked progress in our small surroundings.

YOU have also taken a keen interest in the education of children, which is evinced by your willingness, at all times, to assist our school.

YOUR kindly disposition towards your Bantu employees has won them to your side, so that their loyalty to the City Council and yourself is unquestioned.

WE are thus conferring upon you the honour of possessing a Bantu name, a distinction attained only by merit, and held only by a few Europeans in South Africa. The name is "DUMILZWE" which means "may the story of your kind and sympathetic acts spread the world through". With this name, you are bound to earn the respect of every Bantu.

WE hope that, with the many years of service that are still ahead of you, you will make it a matter of duty always to regard the interests of your Bantu workers as of paramount importance.

MAY God grant you, Mrs. Beagle and your family long life and prosperity.

KHOTSO!   PULA!   NALA!   *Committee*

1. .... *Chairman*   7. ....
2. .... *Secretary*   8. ....
3. ....   9. ....
4. .... *Treasurer*   10. ....
5. .... *Committee*   11. ....
6. ....

Declaration from workers at Bon Accord

Top: Arthur poses with car.
Below: Arthur Beagle on the veldt

Group photo, probably at Bon Accord, Arthur Beagle is seated front and centre

Arthur Beagle (right) and friend, Douglas Leggitt

Arthur and Jessie Beagle, Arthur holding Alan Rutherford, 1949

SOME ADDRESSES
FROM THE BACK OF THE DIARY

Rhina Viljoen
278 Struben St
Pretoria
Mr Conyers & Beattie
115 Plein St August St. Riviera
Vi Smith
25 Voor Rd
Joburg
C.L. Riddle 6895
39 Pretoria St
Krugersdorp
c/o Mrs Warp. Botanic Gdns Co.
or E Hervey Greenacre. M. John
C. Berge 28 Squadron R.F.C.
Italian Exped. Force
F. a. Willmott
Farmer. Rosland
Newcastle
Natal
S Africa

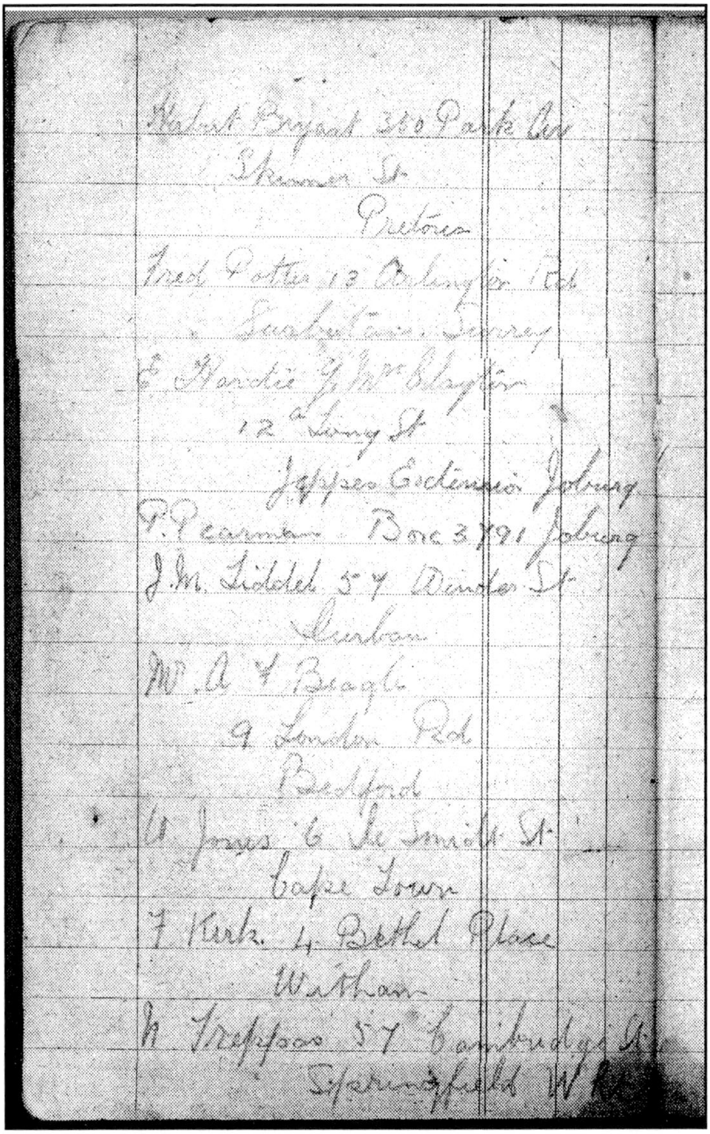

Herbert Bryant 360 Park Av
Skinner St
Pretoria
Fred Potter 13 Arlington Rd
Surbiton. Surrey
E Hardie c/o McClayton
12a Long St
Jeppes Extension Joburg
P. Pearman Box 3791 Joburg
J.M. Liddel 57 Davies St
Durban
Mr. A & Beagle
9 London Rd
Bedford
W Jones 6 De Smidt St
Cape Town
F Kirk. 4 Bethel Place
Witham
R Trepass 57 Cambridge [illegible]
Springfield W [illegible]

Malcolm
Nº 5 Shaft
Crown mines

Wiseman
23   Turf Club St
Turfontein
Thompson & Ballantyne
wit Deep   Feb 26 5
Bellamy P.O. Box 111
Durban Rud G.M.
Riddle 81 Van Leenhof St
or 39 Pretoria St
Krugersdorp

Shaw, Y.W.C.A.
Durban

Ambler 2.8 London Rd
Oldham

Ivy Beagle.
B. Day. 13-4-18

Ernest . H. Jott
Whitecliffe Lane

York

H. Alderman
15 Fairfax Rd
Kelvin Rd
Seacombe
Liverpool

Bearsparke
95 Madeline Rd
Durban

Mr Fred Sharman
90 Bezuidenhout
Troyville
Joburg
Bert Dunsford

Harry G Mrs McFarlan
96 Forrest St
North Perth
W A

A Anderson
13 Millbourn Rd
Bertram
Joburg

Jessie B. D.   {Idia   Redroofs
July 1st.   Southfield
                   House
Mr. Johne
    62 Gable Rd
    Durban.
_____

S. Reynolds
c/o 12 Thomas St
   K. Williams Town
G. Riddlle 6895
   81 Van Leenholf St.
   Krugersdorp.
_____

J. H. Hirst
   21 St James Row
      Burnley
         Lancs
John Midgley
   Crown Mines

D. Hains 5 5 Sawille Rd.
Silvertown London E.
William Scott
37 Silverton St.
Durban   L. Goltman
M. Johns 53 Fourth Av.
Durban
H. Wolfe 482 Schoeman St.
Pretoria
Jas. Bellamy
Durban Roodepoort G.M.C.
P.O. Box 111
Roodepoort,
Transvaal.
Park Hall Cott. Skipton Yorks

John V. du Bruk 329 Frederick St.
Pretoria West.
Bank of National Banks.
Reg No 221. St. Sgt S A S C
(unattached)

THE
EAST AFRICA CAMPAIGN
1916–18

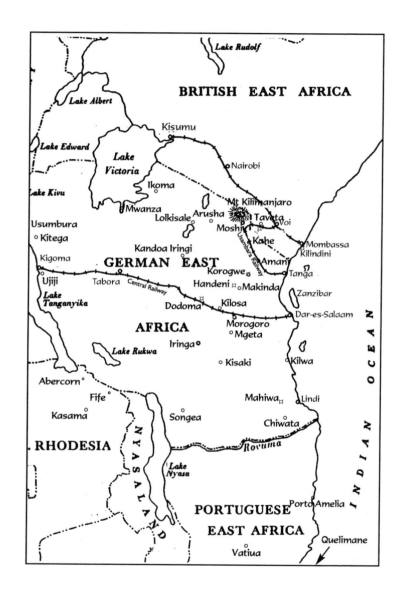

East Africa, 1916–18

EAST AFRICA CAMPAIGN 1916–18
EDITED BY ALAN RUTHERFORD

1916

In January, General Smith-Dorrien, in command of the British forces in East Africa since December 1915, looked to the Committee for Imperial Defence for more men and equipment. His request was blocked by Lord Kitchener, who believed the East African campaign to be little more than a sideshow. The British prime minister eventually consented to sending a British brigade, a South African brigade, 2,000 mounted Boers, a couple of battalions of Indian infantry and twenty-five guns to East Africa, which at this point was being held by two British Battalions, a brigade of the King's African Rifles, about 9,000 Indian troops and some colonial volunteers.

General Smith-Dorrien's original plan was to wait until the rains had stopped, so that he had an army fully prepared and equipped to engage the German forces commanded by General Lettow-Vorbeck. However, Smith-Dorrien fell ill with pneumonia and was hospitalized, and a relapse forced him to return to England. His replacement was a controversial choice, Major General Jan Christian Smuts, an Afrikaaner who had fought with Lord Louis Botha (now the South African prime minister) in the Boer Wars –

fighting the British. After the Boer War Smuts had become a leading cabinet member of the Union of South Africa and now on the eve of his taking command in East Africa he was promoted, to become the youngest Lieutenant General in the British Army.

Smuts arrived in Mombasa on 19 February 1916, just a week after Brigadier General Wilfred Malleson had led an attack on German positions at Salaita, near Taveta. The German force with 1,300 men, two small field guns and twenty-one machine guns had managed to repel a greater force of around 6,000 men. Malleson's attack began on 12 February, opening with a heavy bombardment of what he believed were the German trenches. These proved to be dummy trenches that had been spotted from the air by the newly arrived No.26 Squadron of the Royal Flying Corps (RFC). The German forces (Schutztruppe) were cleverly concealed at the foot of the hill in front of the trenches. When the British began their advance they were laid into by accurate fire from the two field guns and the South Africans came under heavy machine gunfire. The South Africans wavered, and when the German Askaris charged they bolted, leaving guns and equipment to be picked up by the 130th Baluchis, Indian troops, who had, embarrassingly for the White South Africans, witnessed and covered the their flight.

Upon arrival at Mombassa Smuts set off for his headquarters in Nairobi, where he made a brief stop, refusing all the official receptions of the British colonial set, preferring to move south to make a personal reconnaissance of the front in the Serengeti area. Major

General M.J. Tighe, in command of the 2nd Division of East African troops, had drawn up a plan for an attack on German East Africa; Smuts endorsed this with only minor changes. Considerable staff problems arose, with conflicts of opinion and class, due to Smuts' own staff, Smith-Dorrien's staff and Tighe's staff each having been created by the widely differing methods of Colonial, Indian and War Office administrators. Smuts spent little time in sorting out staff problems.

On 5 March, the war began in earnest in East Africa. Smuts launched a two-pronged attack in the Kilimanjaro area. Men under Major General J. M. Stewart, the 1st Division of East African troops, marched to Longido and then southeast around the base of the mountain while Tighe's troops approached west and north of the mountain, through Salaita and Taveta. Smuts' first aim was to advance on and capture the railway beyond Moshi in time to prevent the retreat of German forces under Major Kraut, the same Germans who had routed the South Africans in February. At that time, Smuts armed force consisted of 27,350 combatants including a squadron of the RFC, with seventy-one field guns and 123 machine guns. Using the airfield at Voi, the German lines were reconnoitred by air and their source of water discovered, although this was not attacked, and the town of Salaita was. The Germans had pulled back beyond the Lumi River before the attack began. Moshi was taken next, on 13 March, but still no Germans had been captured or killed. Each time the British attempted to capture or bring Lettow-Vorbeck to battle his army slipped away from them, retreating in the face of overwhelming force, allowing territory to be gained but not squaring up to a decisive battle. And as the Germans retreated, they took away what could be carried and destroyed the rest.

Lettow-Vorbeck now made his base in a plantation on the Usambara railway, the defences of which included one of the Königsberg's guns. As he anticipated, Smuts began to advance down the railway on 18 March heading for Kahe. A pattern emerged which was to be repeated again and again, where almost every time, Lettow-Vorbeck chose the ground where the two forces would meet and trade blows, giving bloody noses to the British before falling back in well-prepared lines. These were guerrilla tactics. At the plantation Smuts found the Germans in strong defensive positions with each flank maintained by two deep, fast-flowing crocodile-infested rivers. The bush, through which the British would have had to advance had been cleared in wide belts to give a clear and deadly field of fire for the German maxims (machine guns). The gun from the Königsberg was sited to cause the maximum destruction. Without hesitating to assess the situation, the British forces pushed forward and suffered heavy casualties. By nightfall they were still pinned down, unable to move. The Germans vanished overnight and the British entered Kahe without opposition, the Königsberg's gun was captured, but it had been made unusable.

Annoyed at these humiliations, Smuts turned on those he thought responsible and sacked Malleson and Stewart, Tighe was sent home after he was assured of a knighthood. Smuts wanted his own men in charge and he now formed three divisions: two under Afrikaaners,

'Jaap' Van Deventer and 'Coen' Brits; the third under Brigadier General A. R. Hoskins, a Staff College graduate and former Inspector General of the King's African Rifles. The plan for German East Africa now became a multi-directional invasion. Brigadier General Northey, in Rhodesia, was to push in from the south. Brigadier General Crewe would cooperate with the Belgians and invade the populated north-west corner of the colony with the Belgians and Smuts would push south-east down the Usambara railway towards Tanga, but turn south towards Handeni and then onto Morogoro. While Van Deventer's division was to push south across the Masai Plain with the key road junction of Kondoa Irangi as his first objective, and then onto the Central Railway. Smuts urged the Portuguese to attack the colony from the south-east.

Smuts misjudged the severity of the rains in his eagerness to bring this camapaign to an end when, in the last week of March, he ordered Van Deventer's 2nd Division to prepare to march on Kondoa Irangi. On 3 April, 1,200 men of the Mounted Brigade splashed out of Arusha in the pouring rain for their destination which was about 200 miles away by the circuitous route they would have to take. In a hard charging attack, the Mounted Brigade forced the surrender of the 28th Field Company at Lolkisale, which was the first serious defeat of the Schutztruppe, and the first German unit to have surrendered. The rain, disease, starvation and exhaustion took a crippling toll on Van Deventer's units. Supply lines were almost non-existent as mud from the heavy rains bogged down all wheeled transport. The situation was dire but they pressed on to Kandoa Irangi.

The Mounted Brigade, several days ahead of the Infantry, found the town deserted and burnt out. A herd of 800 cattle, left by the retreating Germans, was seized upon by the starving troops. The Infantry finally trudged in eleven days after the Mounted Brigade to pick up the scraps. All the units had suffered appallingly in the conditions, and the 2nd Rhodesian were down to fifty fighting men from a strength of 600 three months before. The Germans staged frequent attacks, only too aware of their enemies poor condition.

After the arrival of all of his infantry, Van Deventer who was still outnumbered, stalled. Kraut had 4,000 men in place against Van Deventer's 3,000 troops. The Germans were also in possession of several of the Königsberg's guns, whereas Van Deventer had only a couple of salvaged guns from the Pegasus, which had been sunk in Zanzibar Harbour. The Germans suffered from the rains as well as the British, but they were well supplied by interior lines. On 9th and 10th May the Germans launched four serious attacks on the British forces at Kondoa Irangi. The heaviest weight falling on the 11th and 12th South African Infantry. The attacks, which lasted from 7.30 pm on the 9th until 3.15am on the 10th, were the first, and one of the last times, the Schutztruppe took the offensive against any large segments of Smuts' army. In spite of some tense moments, the South Africans held and the Germans faded away, but Van Deventer's forces were not fit to resume their offensive until the end of June.

In the meantime Smuts launched a two-pronged attack. Brigadier General J. A. Hannyngton moving straight down the railway line at the rate of two miles a day. Brigadier General J. A. Sheppard was in command of a smaller force, moving south-east along the left bank of the Pangani River and then, near Korogwe, turned south towards Handeni. All went well and little opposition was encountered, and on 19 June, some of Sheppard's column marched into Handeni.

The fertile Usambara highlands, where most of the German colonists had settled, were undefended and were easily taken. Amani and the research station there was captured by a British priest named Pearce, now an intelligence officer on Smuts' staff. In spite of the loss of territory, in late April and early May, Lettow-Vorbeck began to receive a stream of fresh supplies from the supply ship, the Marie von Stettin (which had successfully run the British blockade). The ship was loaded to capacity with a list of items that had been smuggled out, its cargo was packed in 60-65 pound parcels, considered suitable for African carriers to carry on their heads. It included four field howitzers, two mountain guns, ammunition (including shells for Königsberg's guns), clothing, tobacco, sweets, equipment of all sorts, medical supplies and other items needed to carry on the campaign. The British ships arrived after the Marie von Stettin's cargo had been unloaded and sunk her with twenty shells. But even this wasn't enough, the ingenius Germans refloated her within a month and she sailed out on a moonless night past two British patrol boats. Almost all the carrier loads from this cargo reached Lettow-Vorbeck.

Handeni, a milestone on the march to Morogoro had been taken, but it was an unhealthy place overrun with rats. When Sheppard's men entered the town they found that Major Kraut and the Germans had only just left the place a few hours before, leaving behind several hundred African carriers who were dying of typhoid. Smuts ignored the plight of the dying Africans and ordered Sheppard's forces on when he heard that Kraut's forces had retired to defensive positions on high ground near Makinda on the Lukigura River. To attack him Smuts formed a flying column under Sheppard that consisted of the 25th Royal Fusiliers (now numbering only 200 men), the 2nd Kashmiri Rifles, the 29th Punjabis, and the 5th and 6th South African Infantry. After a punishing march they arrived before the German positions exhausted and hungry and went straight into battle. The British overran the German positions, capturing a field gun and eight machine guns. They lost ten killed and thirty-six wounded, the Germans lost four Europeans and thirty Africans killed and twenty-one Germans and thirty-two Askaris captured. True to the German guerrilla tactics, most of Kraut's force retreated to fight again another day. The British halted as Lord Louis Botha paid a flying visit to the troops, whilst another Mounted Brigade disembarked at Mombassa. Smuts now approved the doubling in size of the Kings African Rifles (KAR) to 380 officers and 8,100 other ranks.

In the meantime, Tanga was bombarded by three British warships, and on 3 July the town was captured, easing supply problems considerably. With Smuts at

Handeni, Lettow-Vorbeck concentrated his forces at Morogoro on the Central Railway. Kraut made his headquarters at Kilosa 150 miles west of Dar-es-Salaam, and while Smuts planned on German forces defending the railway, Lettow-Vorbeck had no such ideas.

Van Deventer, after building up a two week supply of food and ammunition at Kondoa Irangi and waiting for the country to dry out, resumed his march to the Central Railway. His Mounted Brigade again leading the way and skirmishing with small patrols. Ten days later advanced elements of his force struck the railway at Dodoma, where the local governor surrendered without a shot being fired. Van Deventer then moved south-east along the railway toward Kilosa, reaching it on 22 August, taking it without opposition and establishing his headquarters there. Smuts, however, was coming over difficult overgrown, mountainous and ravine-filled countryside. Lettow-Vorbeck played his usual deadly strategy taking up strong positions, and holding them just long enough to inflict casualties and delay progress. Morogoro was entered by the 2nd Rhodesians on 26 August, just as the German rearguard was leaving south of the town conducting a 'spoiling operation'; ruining supplies, twisting rails and destroying rolling stock. The Central Railway had fallen, but the Schutztruppe was still intact.

For the first eighteen months of the war, the British had been reluctant to commit resources to Africa and refused the Belgians help in mounting an attack on

German East Africa from the Belgian Congo, but once Smuts began to wreak havoc on the German colony, things changed. Relations between the British and Belgians were never that good in Africa, as both were colonial powers in competition for more territory. So it was with great difficulty that a joint invasion effort by British and Belgian forces was finally agreed upon, with the target of Tabora which was now the seat of the German East Africa's government and the headquarters of the Schutztruppe's western command. The Belgian military forces were led by Baron Charles Henri Marie Ernest Tombeur, the British forces in western British East Africa by Sir Charles Preston Crewe. The two men loathed each other, they ignored each other's strategic goals and there was very little cooperation between them.

In March 1916, Tombeur had just over 10,000 men organized into two brigades, one under Colonel Molitor and the other under Lieutenant Colonel F. V. Olsen. They carried sixty machine guns and twelve field guns. The pattern of warfare set here by the Germans followed the highly successful guerrilla pattern set by Lettow-Vorbeck, as they fell back from strong point after strong point inflicting casualties constantly. Olsen occupied Usumbura on the east side of the north end of Lake Tanganyika on 8 June, and marched east to Kitega, capital of Urundi Province. In late June, Molitor's column moving south-west, crossed the Kagera River, turned east towards Lake Victoria, and on 24 June engaged on a three day, hard march to the south-west corner of Lake Victoria.

Crewe planned to capture Mwanza, the key German port at the south end of Lake Victoria. First he sent a flying column to capture Bukoba on the Western shore, but they found the town deserted. The main British force sailed in a fleet of small craft from Kisumu and landed a few miles outside of Mwanza. There was a small, sharp battle, in which another Königsberg gun took part. Before retreating the Germans had managed to destroy the wireless masts, but had done little other damage; almost effortlessly drifting away. Crewe gathered two KAR companies and pursued them, only to become bogged down in marshland.

The Belgians, who had been moving slowly and consolidating their positions, now began a rapid drive south towards Kigoma, the German's chief port on Lake Tanganyika. Crewe also drove south. The advance became a race, but a race slowed by determined and skilled German resistance. The Belgians advanced in two columns, the first column, under the command of Olsen, moving down the east side of the lake took Kigoma, on 28 July. On 2 August they occupied Ujiji, and they now held the western terminus of the Central Railway, down which they moved, toward Tabora. The Germans slowly fell back, destroying the railway as they retreated. After ten days of hard fighting, the Belgians entered Tabora on 19 September 1916. The Germans retreated south-east in three columns, but having achieved their aim of taking Tabora, the Belgians were content and did not pursue the retreating Germans, pleased after capturing a vast tract of land with comparatively small losses.

After spirited opposition and some difficult terrain, Crewe's forces finally got to Tabora six days later.

In Tabora the Allied forces found Governor Schnee's wife, along with another 140 women and a number of children, with 2,000 prisoners of war, mostly British and Belgian, and a few French, Italian and Russian internees. Various charges of abuse and misconduct were levelled against the Germans, but overall the conduct of the Germans and their treatment of the prisoners seems to have been good. By this stage, Lettow-Vorbeck was surrounded by the British, Belgian, Rhodesian and Portuguese troops. It must be remembered that in Africa, as in the trenches of Europe, the most dangerous enemy was disease and it was rife in both theatres. Typhoid, pneumonia, malaria, fleas, worms and blackwater fever being prevalent in Africa, the ratio of non-battle casualties to battle casualties by July 1916 was 31.4 to 1.

Smuts pushed his sick, exhausted and starving troops forward again to catch Lettow-Vorbeck at his headquarters in Morogoro. In his reading of the situation, he took the Germans destruction of every-thing of military value as a sign of the German's demoralization, instead of plain thoroughness. As the troops moved on the village of Kisaki, they found bridges blown, paths blocked and it rained in persistent torrents. Lettow-Vorbeck's troops threw up ambushes and fought stubborn rear guard actions as the pursuit continued. Against Lettow-Vorbeck's 5,000 men the British were now fielding about 80,000. Another 4,500 men were in German service but not under Lettow-Vorbeck's direct personal command. Dar-es-Salaam was captured on 3 September and the British found everything of value destroyed, the Germans had left 370 civilians and eighty hospital patients for the British to care for, the only slight triumph was the destruction of another of the Königsberg's guns.

By September, both sides had fought themselves to a standstill, the Germans were in just as bad a shape as the British. The Schutztruppe fell back to Mgeta, leaving behind a hospital full of sick and wounded at Kisaki for the British to care for. The German forces were now reduced to 1,100 Europeans and 7,300 Askaris with seventy-three machine guns, sixteen field guns and four of the Königsberg's 105mm guns. Smuts' force ground to halt completely exhausted and depleted at Kisaki, despite Smuts' order to carry on they could not, and reluctantly he had to agree.

Smuts sent Governor Schnee a demand for surrender, offering to meet Lettow-Vorbeck and Schnee at a time and place to be agreed upon. The last three months of 1916 saw no more offensive operations by Smuts, he moved his headquarters to Dar-es-Salaam and, at last, worked to get his supply lines functioning. He also ordered all those declared medically unfit to be sent home, a belated, but welcome, gesture from Smuts who privately was worried he may gain the nickname 'butcher'. The mass exodus of 12,000 men from the force was replaced by Nigerians and the 2nd Gold Coast regiment.

DISEASE TO STARVATION: "My best friend ! You're doing wonders."
(The *Rand Daily Mail*, 14 November 1916)

The press in South Africa had until now been supportive and followed the official line about reporting on the war, but when increasing reports of the worsening conditions in East Africa reached them, to their credit, they spoke out.

What had been achieved so far had been at severe cost. Since 22 May, when columns marched out of Kahe, 28,000 oxen had died on the three month trek to Morogoro. Vast herds had been commandeered to keep pace with needs, and what was yet to come would defy imagination in its disregard for animal life – and this was a contributory cause for the famine that was the legacy of this war amongst the local people during and after it. Everywhere these armies rampaged in East Africa, they took and devoured anything edible and left the countryside barren – the survival of local people was secondary to the war effort. During World War 1 animals were still the main means of transport and they were expendable, their only medication were injections of arsenic for tsetse fly and a bullet in the brain. In another three month period Smuts' army lost 11,000 oxen, 10,000 horses, 10,000 mules and 2,500 asses through overwork, disease and want of grain – and this waste continued, for here in East Africa the Black African carriers were also considered expendable.

During the imposed inaction of the last three months of 1916, Smuts sent out another pincer movement. A force under Brigadier General J. A. Hannyngton with the North Lancashires, two Indian brigades and two battalions of the King's African Rifles by ship to Kilwa, from there they moved inland in an attempt to get behind the enemy's lines. Lettow-Vorbeck was aware of this, and drew back to the Rufiji. His main concern at that time was the withdrawal of Wahle's three columns from Tabora, which were trying to join forces with Kraut in the fertile Mahenge area.

Kraut with about 2,000 men was now pressing on Northey's northernmost positions near Iringa in the Southern Highlands, 110 miles south of Dodoma. In late October, the Germans had cut off the town, ambushed a relief column and cut it to pieces, snapped up several supply dumps, raided Northey's line of communications, and then launched a vigorous attack on Iringa itself. The attack had failed and one of Wahle's columns was trapped and forced to surrender. In all Wahle suffered about 750 casualties in his withdrawal from Tabora to the Mahenge area.

A small force of Germans were discovered holding a region between Tabora and Lake Ruka and on 22 November it was cornered by Murray's column – over 300 prisoners were captured, of whom 249 were Askaris. All of the German forces were now in the southern half of the colony, and for the first time Lettow-Vorbeck now began to suffer serious supply problems of his own. The southern reaches of German East Africa were more primitive than the northern provinces, and the locals were not pleased by the presence of the Schutztruppe. The British, taking advantage of the German's predicament, arranged a coordinated uprising for their benefit. Lettow-Vorbeck failed to capture Kibata after six weeks of hard fighting in December, and so failed to gain access to the British supplies there and was forced to withdraw into a wilderness area just north of the Rufiji.

1917

On 20 January 1917, Smuts handed over command to Major General A. R. Hoskins and departed first for South Africa and then for England, where he had been invited to attend the Imperial War Conference. Smuts, despite his errors of judgment, pushing his forces to the limits of endurance, and gaining only territory and no decisive victory, had returned to South Africa to a hero's welcome. By the end of January he had been restored to his family at Doornkloof, and then it was off to the War Office in England. By the time he reached London, Smuts was declaring that the war in East Africa was over and that he had won it. This was news to Hoskins, and the starving soldiers in the bush, who was now under pressure to bring the campaign to an end, vainly trying to explain that the German army in the field had not been defeated. The rains added to his troubles, coming early in 1917 – within five days of Smuts leaving – it was said that the rains were the worst in living memory! The Nigerians and the Cape corps were at once cut off. Every ounce of food, for rations were soon to be measured in ounces, had to be carried nearly a hundred miles by carriers waist-deep in water. Pack animals died after a single journey, and there were so few transport drivers that hundreds of Fords stood idle for days with no one capable of driving them. Soon the real nightmare really began, as Captain Downes records:

'Men driven by hunger started to dig up roots, or picked herbs, with disasterous results. Crime became common as men raided supply dumps for rice and biscuits. Many died from eating poisoned roots. So acute became the need that some resorted to digging up the rotting bodies of pack animals. A temporary bridge was brought down when famished men cut the rawhide strips binding the spars. The hides were cooked down into soup, and so disposed of by the starving men... Back on the Rufiji a bottle of brandy from a dead officer's effects was sold for £10 and an NCO's toothbrush for £1.13s.4d. Officers were eating roasted jungle rats and monkey brains.'

In spite of Smuts' remarks, Hoskins did make some progress. He brought in some reforms, and he realized that Black Africans made better bush soldiers than the White Africans, Indians or Europeans. He ordered a rapid expansion of the KAR, Hoskins tripled Smuts' final KAR strength of 8,000. Before the end of the war there were 35,000 KAR, commanded by European Officers, with European NCOs, whose numbers were also increased. Hoskins was able to guarantee the numbers of carriers, the forgotten and unsung (reluctant) heroes of this campaign, with the compulsory service acts now coming into force in Africa. This new legislation enabled the virtual enslavement of tens of thousands of Black African carriers, taken from their families to face disease, overwork, and most likely, death – all for a cause little understood, or had sympathy for.

Nowhere in Smuts' report to their Lordships in London, or subsequent reports from the field is any mention made of the contribution made by the carriers, often nameless, mainly coerced, black Africans. The British source was inexhaustible from neighbouring colonial territories, but the Germans were limited to those they could pick up along the way. They were accused of kidnapping and manacling carriers, abandoning and even shooting those too ill to continue. Of those serving the British forces, a staggering 45,000 carriers died of disease and neglect, 376 were killed and 1,645 were wounded. And of those serving the Germans, between 6,000 and 7,000 men, women and children (carriers were often accompanied by their families) died from wounds or sickness.

Not only in East Africa was there this terrible waste of life amongst the carriers, who were regarded, like the horses and mules, totally expendable, but many returning to Durban in the last stages of dysentery and fever died at sea, where not only their bodies, but also their identity discs, were thrown overboard – as if they never existed! Their families were left to wonder their fate. Little was ever recorded of these men, but in the book, *They Fought for King and Kaiser*, Private Frank Reid of the 9th, a maxim gunner, recalls carriers who carried and serviced his gun:

'They were called *bom-bom boys*, they carried the gun, ammunition, spare-parts box, the tripod and the water-can for cooling the barrel. There were about a dozen to each gun and a few more to carry their groundsheets and blankets. They carried their loads on their heads on a circular pad of twisted grass. Their necks were strong, but they could not get the loads on to their heads without help.'

Reid's Native Machine-gun Porters (their official title) were named Gertie, Piano, Wall Eye and Magoo. Others were nameless. According to Reid, in an ambush that wiped out most of his gun team 'their black and battered bodies were found in the grass near the spot.'

Hoskins was relieved of command after less than four months, being sent to Mesopotamia to command a division. Some believed the reasons for Hoskins relief were politically motivated and due in some way to Smuts at the War Office; Smuts misguidedly believed the East Africa campaign almost over and wanted it to be remembered as a South African victory. The South African, Van Deventer, replaced Hoskins. This was a man who saw the true objective, not a geographical location, but the destruction of the German Army in the field. But even with Hoskins' preparations and the ceasing of the rains, Van Deventer was still not able to mount a major offensive for more than three months. It was during this time, that Lettow-Vorbeck forced the German refugees draining his resources to cross the river and be found by the British – draining their resources instead of his. However, the African women did not go, they walked only a few miles before stopping, eating all their rations, and humiliating their escort by walking back to camp. The German commander, had, by now, trained his own men to live off the land as the Askaris did.

In February 1917 something odd happened. Without orders, Captain Max Wintgens, a professional officer of great ability, broke away from the force under Kraut and struck off on his own. He took with him about 700 Askaris, several hundred carriers, three small field guns and thirteen machine guns. Both sides were surprised. His purpose was, and still is unclear, but presumably based on the idea of tying up more British troops. His force moved at a rapid pace clearing the country of all supplies as they moved, and thus ensuring that any pursuit would have to be supplied from the rear. The British troops following this maverick officer and his men were brought to a standstill by this tactic. It seemed, at first, as though they were heading for Rhodesia, but instead they turned north and west through territory the Allies had thought was safely under their control. Murray's column was the first to take up the chase, but was 200 miles behind. Some of the units that did catch up with Wintgens' renegades were treated harshly, and a KAR detachment that got in the way was badly cut up. Northey called for help and Hoskins sent Major H. G. Montgomerie with 300 men from Morogoro to Tabora, most of them were captured German Askaris who had been 'persuaded' to change sides – these 'turncoat' troops still had to be given orders in German. Montgomerie's force moved out but his force was too small to do more than keep track of Wintgens' movements.

So seriously did the British view this development that Van Deventer created a special force to deal with Wintgens (EDFORCE), commanded by Brigadier General W. F. S. Edwards with a force of a KAR battalion (Montgomerie), the 130th Baluchis, 400 men of the Cape Corps and fifty mounted Askaris – in all 1,700 rifles and 14 machine guns. Edwards established his headquarters at Tabora and the Belgians, their newly gained possessions threatened, agreed to cooperate. On 23 May, the 6th Belgian Battalion captured Wintgens, who had contracted typhus and

surrendered himself to get treatment, but would not
surrender his troops. Lieutenant Heinrich Naumann
took command of the column, and proved himself as
capable and resourceful at Wintgens. South Africa
answered Van Deventer's request for more troops
by raising the 10th South African Horse and sending
it to East Africa. The Nigerians soon joined in, and
soon there was a brigade each of Belgian and British
troops, nearly 4,000 men, in pursuit of fewer than 500
Askaris led by a German lieutenant.

On 26 May, a Nigerian regiment moving west from
Morogoro on the Central Railway, stopped to take on
water and wood fuel about sixty miles south-east of
Tabora. At this time, Naumann was crossing the
railway through a culvert less than two miles away.
He sent out patrols down the tracks to both sides of
his crossing point and one clashed with a Nigerian
patrol. When a stronger Nigerian force came up in
response, it found a British railway repair crew and,
thinking they were the Germans, exchanged fire with
them while the real German force slipped away. Two
weeks later, a British aeroplane dropped darts on
the Nigerians; the pilot claimed he had mistaken
them for the German column. Stories of the Germans
atrocities grew ever more horrifying as rumours
circulated that Naumann planned to invade British
East Africa. Naumann raided Kahe at the end of
August, burning stores, looting trains and wrecking
the station there. The Belgians found and attacked
Naumann at Ikoma, but were out manouvered and
were only saved by the arrival of Major Drought and
his 'Skin Corps' (the Cape Corps). Naumann was

finally surrounded on 30 September close to the British East Africa border near Kilimanjaro by 4 KAR, the South African Horse and the Cape Corps. He surrendered on 2 October; he still had 14 Europeans, 165 Askaris and 250 carriers.

Meanwhile in June, the country had dried out and the 3 KAR, with the Gold Coast regiment, had engaged a force of Germans led by Captain Eberhard von Lieberman, and, after sustaining casualties had driven the Germans back with a vicious bayonet attack. On 2 August, the British staged a three-pronged attack on Lettow-Vorbeck's main position. But this had not been properly reconnoitred and was repulsed. During the attack, a German force had slipped behind their lines and attacked the British supply column.

Lettow-Vorbeck was promoted to the rank of Major General during the Kaiser's speech on the third anniversary of the war.

In September 1917, Van Deventer finally announced that the 'situation is ripe for the main advance... . Sufficient motor transport is at this time available for the whole force.' On 10 September, he moved his headquarters south to Kilwa and nine days later his major offensive began. A force from Lindi advanced south-west while another from Kilwa pushed south, threatening the Germans flank and rear. With overwhelmingly superior manpower and adequate supplies and transport, both forces made progress moving constantly until December. Just one hitch came in October, the last big battle and bloodiest of the entire campaign was fought in the bush about forty-five miles up the Lukuledi River from Lindi at a place called Mahiwa, which later gave its name to the battle. The Germans were positioned on a ridge behind the dry bed of a small stream. The British began their attack at daybreak on 17 October and the fighting continued throughout the day. It was a battle of trenches and dugouts, grenades and machine guns, of bayonet charges, of blood, mud and all the awful classic features of the Western Front.

The British forces were commanded by Brigadier General Gordon Beves, Lettow-Vorbeck had gambled correctly on Beves throwing his troops into a frontal attack much the same as he had done at the battle of Reata on 11 March 1916. He strengthened his centre and placed it under Wahle who had recently joined him. The Nigerians were badly shaken by German shellfire which had hit their shallow trenches three times in quick succession. The night of 17–18 October was relatively quiet.

The battle was renewed in full fury at first light. The Germans concentrated on a gap between two columns and the last remnant of the 25th Royal Fusiliers was nearly annihilated trying to stem it. By nightfall of the second day, both sides fell back exhausted with heavy casualties. The British had lost more than half their men, 2,700 out of 4,900 men. German losses were ninety-five killed and 422 wounded out of 1,500 combatants. Lettow-Vorbeck, unlike the British, could not replace his losses and was forced to withdraw. Charges of brutality and murder where laid against the German Askaris who were accused of bayoneting wounded men as they were crawling to places of safety.

Seriously hampered by supply problems and with the British in pursuit, Lettow-Vorbeck decided to invade Portuguese Africa. He had supplies for six weeks, one Königsberg gun (still!) and a captured Portuguese mountain gun, but only 400,000 rounds of ammunition, most of which was for the old 1871 pattern smoking rifles.

Lettow-Vorbeck left all his sick and wounded at a place called Chiwata (ninety-eight Germans and 425 Askaris) and headed for the Rovuma River, which was the border between German and Portuguese East Africa. When the British entered Chiwata they freed 121 prisoners of war who had been captured at Tanga in November 1914. As the Germans moved on they left behind more sick and wounded. Max Loof, the captain of the Königsberg was left behind, Lettow-Vorbeck would also have liked to dump Schnee, but the governor was proving durable.

Lettow-Vorbeck's force was now down to the best and fittest, 200 Europeans and 2,000 Askaris planned to join up with Captain Theodor Tafel's force heading south from Mahenge. But British Intelligence discovered that Tafel's force had a severe supply problem and they destroyed all supplies on his route. For some unknown reason, Tafel's column turned off when only a mile from Lettow-Vorbeck. The day after

Lettow-Vorbeck crossed the Rovuma, Tafel attacked
a detachment of Indian troops inflicting heavy
casualties. The next day a portion of Tafel's column
surrendered. The following day, amazingly Tafel
destroyed all his weapons and surrendered the
remainder of his column, a total of ninety-five
Europeans and 1,200 Askaris with all their carriers
surrendered to some 100 Indian soldiers who they
had just routed. Tafel had concluded that Lettow-
Vorbeck had abandoned him, when in fact, he was
less than a days march away. Lettow-Vorbeck never
considered surrender, and when the news came with
a few men who hadn't surrendered, it was a severe
and unexpected blow.

Lettow-Vorbeck waded across the Rovuma on 25
November 1917 and entered Portuguese territory.
Even before they were across they engaged a
Portuguese force of about a thousand men who had
come up to prevent the crossing. The Germans and
their Askaris slaughtered them, barely two or three
hundred survived. Portugese supply dumps fell into
Lettow-Vorbeck's hands, including food, six British
machine guns, enough new Portuguese rifles to equip
half his forces and 250,000 rounds of ammunition. The
Portuguese Askaris were taken prisoner and
converted into carriers and the advance continued.
The Portuguese fell at every turn, another bonus was
once they crossed the river Governor Schnee became
silent, no longer having authority over Lettow-
Vorbeck. The British sent an officer under a flag of
truce to inform Schnee that his colony had formally
been declared an Allied protectorate.

The first Zeppelin making a trial run to east Africa was struck by lightning and destroyed. A second Zeppelin was sent on 21 September to East Africa with the intention of resupplying Lettow-Vorbeck with 15 tons of ammunition bush knives, binoculars and other useful items. The entire Zeppelin was built to be torn apart for useful items when it arrived. It was ordered to return to Bulgaria when over the Sudan by the German Admiralty, which had false information of Lettow-Vorbeck's defeat. No more Zeppelin flights were attempted, although it would appear the Schutztruppe needed no such help – the Portuguese maintained well-supplied, badly defended supply depots.

December 1917 saw the Germans in the centre of a group of Portuguese plantations, amidst provision of all sorts. On Christmas day the Germans ate roast pork and drank Portuguese wines, ending the feast with real coffee and cigars. Portuguese East Africa was a haven for the Germans, the natives welcoming them with open arms. The Schutztruppe was now divided into units, each consisting of three companies, a field hospital and a supply train. The subordinate commanders, when detached or in advance of the main force, were given wide discretionary powers. The Schutztruppe routinely marched two hours and rested for a half hour, in this fashion a marching column could cover fifteen, even twenty miles in six hours. At midday they halted for lunch, a foreign notion to the Africans but many adopted it. Still, the Askaris' women and children marched with the columns. The carriers loads were about twenty-five kilograms (fifty-five lbs) and they marched barefoot, if stuck by a thorn they cut it out. British aircraft showered the Schutztruppe with leaflets in Swahili inducing desertion with money, food and more. Some deserted, most did not and even some of the deserters returned and were welcomed back. British and Portuguese prisoners marched with the column in good humour, although the Portuguese were disdained by the others, their health bad, their equipment poor from lack of care and their senior officer complained constantly.

1918

Early in 1918, Van Deventer sent Lettow-Vorbeck a demand for his surrender. This only strengthened the Germans belief that his escape from German East Africa had taken the British by surprise.

No area in the Portuguese territory offered the German forces the resources needed for a long occupation, so Wahle was sent off with a sizeable force westward and Captain Franz Köhl led another detached force toward the east coast while Lettow-Vorbeck remained with the main body south, up the valley of the Lujenda River and on into country almost unknown to Europeans, where he found an elevated, fertile land with a healthy climate – an ideal country for a guerrilla force.

Van Deventer was presented by a new set of problems, most of which revolved around obstructive Portuguese officials and the primitive conditions

within the colony itself. Portuguese blessing was
finally given and British troops landed at Porto Amelia
and two columns were sent inland. One commanded
by Lieutenant Colonel George Gifford and the other
under Lieutenant Colonel R. A. de B. Rose, who had
served in the Cameroons campaign.

On 12 April, Gifford's column, composed entirely of
KAR battalions, collided with Köhl's column near a
place called Medo. There was considerable confusion
and Medo was a soldier's battle of ambushes and
fighting at close quarters – taking place in exceed-
ingly difficult country, thick jungle where roads were
mere tunnels through bamboo thicket and elephant
grass. At this season long stretches of the road were
more suitable for boats.

The first six months of the last year of the war saw
many small fights, but Medo aside, only one battle of
major importance. Near Korewa, amidst rocky hills
and thick bush on 22 May, the British almost accom-
plished what they had often tried to do; surround a
major portion of the Schutztruppe. German casualties
were not high, but Köhl's column which was the unit
attacked, had not yet recovered from the indecisive
battle at Medo and now lost all its transport, 100,000
rounds of small arms ammunition, the last sixty-seven
rounds for the Portuguese mountain gun, and large
quantities of medical supplies, food and baggage.
Schnee, who was with Koehl, also lost his baggage.

On 1 June, Lettow-Vorbeck crossed the broad Lurio
River near Vatiua. He then pushed south through

extremely rugged country where steep hills rose in every direction out of a tangle of near impenetrable bush. Pursued by a heavy Portuguese column and six British columns, the smallest of which was at battalion strength, he fought numerous rearguard actions. Desperate for food and supplies, the Schutztruppe attacked and captured Alto Molocue, a Portuguese administrative and supply centre, where they acquired a herd of pigs (soon turned into sausages, and 75,000 lbs of foodstuffs. Not long after, on 1–3 July, they captured the town of Nhamacurra, where they picked up two field guns and a few shells. By chance, when a steamer on the river innocently landed, they found on board a British doctor with a much-needed load of medical supplies, including quinine.

At the nearby railway station, they fought a swift bloody battle and drove off the Allied defenders. They gained 350 rifles, ten machine guns, 300,000 kilograms of food and enough clothing for everyone. The troops were allowed to drink all the wine they could, for it could not be hauled away – there was just too much of it. Lettow-Vorbeck allowed the Allies to get between him and what they thought was his objective, Quelimane, a major port to the south. He gave his troops a rest, then headed north leaving the British behind in their hastily improvised defences. A British column, still marching south, was caught out by the unpredictable Germans, and on 24 August, there was a sharp fight at Namarroe when a German column under Captain Erich Müller encountered a detachment of the 2/4th KAR. A week later, at a place called Lioma, Lettow-Vorbeck narrowly escaped

capture by three battalions of the KAR, but still lost
about 250 dead and 48,000 rounds of ammunition, the
KAR also lost heavily.

With the way back to Rovuma clear, the world was hit by
the second of three waves of influenza and both sides
were struck down with heavy numbers of sick. The
Germans eventually staggered back into German East
Africa and marched towards Tabora, capturing a few
supply depots helped their health improve, but the
Askaris and carriers began to desert. At Songea
Lettow-Vorbeck's advance guard ran into strong
opposition, and he turned westward. In Mid-October
the Germans passed around the north end of Lake
Nyasa and invaded Northern Rhodesia. Again they
left behind their sick and wounded, which included
Kurt Wahle, who was strapped to a litter.

Although lacking adequate maps, Lettow-Vorbeck
and his men marched towards Fife, just over the
border in Northern Rhodesia. Although a column of
KAR raced to beat him there, he arrived first but
found Fife strongly defended and moved on, taking a
nearby mission station where he appropriated
fourteen kilograms of quinine. His remaining troops,
now almost sensing the hopelessness of their
situation, trudged on, reaching Kajambi on 6
November, with a force of 750 KAR guided by a
Rhodesian settler following in the their rear. Most of
Van Deventer's troops were at Tabora and along the
northern railway. Lettow-Vorbeck's entire strategy
was, for the first time, wholly concerned with the need
for supplies and food. On 9 November his advance

guard captured Kasama where they acquired a little ammunition and a considerable supply of European food. On 12 November, the Germans and British fought a final skirmish on a river bank near Kasama. On 13 November, Lettow-Vorbeck received a note from Van Deventer telling him of the Armistice. It was confirmed by tapping the telephone lines of the British.

The last of the Schutztruppe marched into Abercorn on 25 November, and at noon, the brief ceremony of surrender took place.

The defeat of Imperial Germany robbed the Germans of all their African possessions. The Schutztruppe emerged undefeated from the African war, admired by their opponents as the most efficient and effective fighting force seen on the continent of Africa during the Great War. Lettow-Vorbeck left Africa on 17 January 1919, five years to the day since he had arrived, with 114 Germans soldiers and sailors, 107 women and eighty-seven children bound for Cape Town and Rotterdam.

The European armies packed up, the South Africans, Nigerians and others returned home – leaving behind a spoiled countryside devoid of domestic animals or staple foodstuffs – a legacy for famine which claimed thousands of lives in the years that followed.

Additional information from
James Paul at http://british-forces.com

SOME NOTES

Lettow-Vorbeck, General Paul Emil von. (1870–1964) Born
Saarlouis, Germany. Sent to China with the German
Expeditionary Force, Lettow-Vorbeck saw action in the
Boxer Rebellion, served in Namibia (German South West
Africa) during the Hottentot and Herero Rebellion of
1904–08, and wounded, was sent for several months to
South Africa for recuperation.

As a Lieutenant-Colonel in February, 1914, he was
appointed commander of the forces in German East
Africa, with a dozen companies of Askari troops. In
August, 1914, effectively isolated from outside command,
Lettow-Vorbeck launched a series of raids against the
British railway in Kenya, fought off a British amphibious
attack on Tanga and captured large amounts of arms and
ammunitions to supply his troops. Lettow-Vorbeck
managed to salvage the guns from the destroyed ship
Königsberg, and was able to use these along with guerilla
tactics to hold off the offensive of Lieutenant General Jan
Christian Smuts in March, 1916. He remained continually
on the offensive, gradually working south, he officially
surrendered to the British, having never been defeated, on
25 November 1918. Lettow-Vorbeck never had more than
approximately 12,000 troops at his disposal, but tied down
as many as ten to twenty times that number of Allied
troops.

In Germany he was given a hero's welcome, and he remained in the army, later to suppress a Communist uprising in Hamburg. He became a politician and served for 10 years in the Reichstag. He and Smuts formed a lasting friendship and he sat next to Smuts as guest of honour at the anniversary dinner of the East African Expeditionary Force.

Von Lettow-Vorbeck by Santana

After World War Two, in which he opposed the Nazis, he lived in poverty for many years. Smuts, on hearing of his plight, sent him regular food parcels.

Lettow-Vorbeck died in 1964.

Smuts, Field-Marshal, Jan Christian. (1870–1950). Jan Christian Smuts was born 24 May 1870 near Riebeeck West in what is now South Africa. He was educated at Victoria College in Stellenbosch and later studied law at Cambridge. He returned to South Africa after his studies at Cambridge in 1895. As a result of the Jameson Raid his political leanings turned from endorsement of Cecil Rhodes' dream of a British Africa to support of President Paulus Kruger and the South African Republic and he was appointed State Attorney for the South African Republic.

In the Boer War Smuts led a Boer unit in the area of Vereeniging and Potchefstroom and later led an expedition into the Cape Colony. He participated in the meetings at Vereeniging and was there when the surrender was signed at the end of May 1902.

After the elections of February 1907, Smuts became part of Prime Minister Louis Botha's cabinet. In May 1910, the Union of South Africa was achieved under a constitution Smuts helped to write.

World War 1, and in February 1916, now Lieutenant-General Smuts, he took command of the Allied forces in East Africa. Here he enthusiastically entered the chase for Colonel Paul Lettow-Vorbeck, who evaded capture even to the end of the war.

In January 1917 Lieutenant-General Smuts turned over command and left for England where he had been appointed a member of the Imperial War Cabinet. He resigned the War Cabinet in December 1918 and in late

June 1919 he and Premier Botha signed the Treaty of Versailles.

After the death of Premier Botha in 1919, Smuts became Premier of South Africa and remained so until 1924. In September 1939 he was again Premier and was Commander-in-Chief of the South African and Rhodesian Forces from 1940–1945. In September 1941 he was awarded the rank of Field Marshal. When the war ended in Europe in 1945, Premier Smuts was in San Francisco working with other delegates on the United Nations Charter.

Smuts by Santana

Field Marshal Jan Christian Smuts died at home in South Africa on 11 September 1950.

Van Deventer, Sir Jacob Louis 'Jaap' (1874–1922)
He moved to the Transvaal as a young man and became a gunner in the Transvaal State Artillery in 1896. In 1899 he married Prinsina Booysen and they had two sons and three daughters. He was active during the Boer War and is credited with having fired the first shot of the war at Kraaipan on 12 October 1899. He rose quickly through the ranks and became a column commander in General Smuts' raid into the Cape Province. He ended the war as combat-general, second only to Smuts in the Cape, and with a throat injury which caused permanent hoarseness.

At the outbreak of World War 1 Colonel Van Deventer served in the SA Staff Corps, then in October 1914 he commanded the force which quelled the rebellion under General 'Manie' Maritz. He was then involved in the South West Africa campaign; as brigadier-general he commanded the 1st South African Mounted Brigade. In December 1915 he left for German East Africa, where he waged the campaign against General Von Lettow-Vorbeck until November 1918.

Van Deventer was promoted Major General and knighted KCB, becoming known as 'Sir Jaap'. After the war he was placed on the retired list and in 1920 he became ADC to King George V.

He was recalled in 1922 to assist in suppressing the Rand Miners' revolt and commanded the area from Germiston to Benoni. He died on 27 August 1922 of heart failure.